"Teachers are not min[illegible] know what our stuc[illegible] they don't know."

The tric[illegible] with sharing what t[illegible] that asking questic[illegible] a sign of stupidity. Helping them overcome their fears and setting them on the path of lifelong learning is easy.

This book offers strategies to empower children to embrace what they don't know and have it work for them. It also demonstrates how students can be trained to get their needs met from every teacher they encounter.

This book is for you if:

- You have students who fail to complete homework.
- You have students who procrastinate.
- You have students whose desks look like they threw up.
- You have parents who feel the need to do your students' projects.
- You have students who take regular trips to "Lala Land."

This book is for you if:

- You want to spend less time teaching with better results.
- You want to do less reteaching.
- You want to empower your students to become their own advocates.
- You want your students to feel comfortable sharing what they do not know.
- You want your students to perform well on standardized tests.
- You want students who turn work in on time.

What Do Children Say About This Approach?

- "The students in seventh grade who learned "Proper Prior Planning to Prevent Poor Performance" haven't any problem with planning projects. The students who didn't are having a really hard time. Learning how to plan so we didn't need our parents' help was one of the best things we learned in third grade." *Melody*
- "It felt good being able to decide when and where I got to do my homework." *Taylor*
- "I know how to get my work done without my mom telling me and that makes me feel good." *Zach*
- "I was glad you pushed me to try, because I would never have known I could solve the problems by myself if you hadn't." *Tash*
- "Now I know I need to draw pictures in order to remember what I have to learn." *Katelyn*
- "When I was doing my homework I started to get frustrated, and then I remembered some of the tricks for figuring out the problem. I took a mental trip back to the classroom, and I could figure out the problem. I don't think I will get as frustrated next time." *Bryan*
- "Now I know that it is important to tell the teacher what I don't know, so she knows what I don't know. I don't feel stupid when I ask a question anymore." *Charles*
- "I learned never to hand Ms. O a paper that she hasn't asked for because if she loses it, it will be my fault, because she warned us that she loses papers." *Brett*
- "I used to think that I was dumb if I made mistakes. Mistakes just tell me what I don't know. Now I find out why I made the mistake. Sometimes the paper is graded wrong and I get a better score." *Jason*
- "I never had to listen before. If I don't listen now, I will have trouble with the homework." *Jared*
- "My mom used to try to tell me how to study and it didn't work. Now she sees that I have to study differently." *Jo*
- "Making note cards and studying them a little each night just before bed helps me remember my vocabulary easily." *Kori*

Homework Solutions:

A Teacher's Guide

The Missing Link Between Home and School

Victoria Olivadoti

"Homework Solutions"™ of Victoria Olivadoti
ISBN:0-9713302-4-7

Cover designed by Teresa London of London Associates
Illustrations by Shelly Olivadoti

For more information, contact:
Tori Publishing
10932 El Coco Circle
Fountain Valley, CA 92708
714 964-6353
www.homeworkdoc.com

The Biggest Mistakes Offer the Greatest Opportunities

Does this desk look familiar?

This is a desk of a child who needs the program you are about to learn. The owners of desks like this one need our help and compassion. If they knew how to do it differently, they would. After all, they would also like to receive a goodie for being caught with a tidy desk, but that will not happen unless the teacher catches the desk within an hour of it being cleaned. Try hard as they might, these students try to keep it together. They just do not have a natural ability to keep materials organized, manage time or get a paper to and from school in one piece. They suffer from paper and time management dysfunction. This book is for them.

If you are a teacher whose desk always looks organized and you can find a paper at the drop of a hat, you may have difficulty understanding these children. What comes easily for some people is tremendously stressful for others. Showing compassion for these students and offering the strategies found in this book will help reduce their stress. Judging them and calling them lazy will only add to what is already a stressful situation.

If your favorite saying is "It's here somewhere," you understand how frustrating this dysfunction can be. It is a life-long challenge, but it is manageable if training starts early in a child's education.

Dedication

I dedicate this book to my father, Bill Matzkin, and my mother, Phyllis Matzkin, and my children, Shelly Olivadoti-Santoro and Melissa Olivadoti.

My father was an incredibly talented and determined man. He was not afraid to express an opposing opinion on issues of importance to him. He was a visionary and could determine when and where change needed to be made. As a result of his controversial ideas, my father was not always the most popular person. But after the dust settled, it was often clear that he was correct. Many grew to trust his opinions.

Opposition did not stop him, because he always had the courage of his convictions. He also understood the law of abundance and knew if he was following his intuition, he would be okay. Nothing was beyond his ability. His motto was "If you end up with lemons, make some lemonade." He would not accept pity from anyone. Instead, he encouraged his children and grandchildren to be a part of the solution.

My mother is a young, vibrant woman. She has overcome tremendous adversity and proved to me that it is not what happens to you, it is how you deal with it that matters. She taught me valuable skills of organization that did not come naturally to me. Her love of life is infectious and our times together are always filled with laughter and intense conversations. I never doubted that my mother felt I could accomplish anything to which I put my mind. Many times I overcame obstacles simply because I knew she believed I could.

My oldest daughter, Shelly, is very creative and created the stick figures for this book. She taught me about giving up power to empower her. Her drive and determination are infectious. Watching her travel the world has been an inspiration to me. Many of the lessons in this book came from parenting. I gained a whole new perspective on education after becoming the parent of a strong-willed child.

My daughter, Melissa, has taught me more than any one person. Melissa helped me realize that I needed to be her parent, not her teacher. This was difficult for the teacher in me. Through interactions with her, I developed the home program for communication that parents can implement to empower their children. She helped me realize that my role was to teach her how to communicate her needs to her teachers. At the same time, she helped me to hone my listening skills. Melissa, who is also a neuro scientist, offered her extensive knowledge about the brain to assure the accuracy of this book. She has shown how someone can take a personal life challenge and become a part of the solution instead of a victim of circumstances. Her research will change lives.

Both of my children have proven that when you give your children power over their own lives, they will makes choices from which they will learn and your relationship with them will be loving and rewarding.

Acknowledgements

Homework Solutions is more than a homework program. It is the realization of a dream. The dream is to help students and teachers find joy in learning. It is to demonstrate the ease with which students can improve their performance while realizing their strengths and strengthening their weaknesses. The dream is also to reduce the needless stress experienced in homes today. Through this program the parent's' role shifts and the child becomes empowered.

It is because of the help and encouragement of many people that this book exists. Twelve years ago, Karen Wells begged me to print my first book, *Homework Solutions for Weary Parents*. My countless students became my "lab rats," as noted by Danie Diamond, a former student. They have provided me with reality checks when I thought I had a good idea. Their enthusiasm for the power they gain through this program has motivated me to share the power with other teachers.

I owe a debt of gratitude to my colleagues, Elaine Sarkin and Karen Connor, who embraced the program and provided amazing support and encouragement. Without the support of Dr. Laura Hathaway, I would never have been able to implement this program. Her vision has created a wonderful future for hundreds of students, and she has given me wings and allowed me to take flight. John Sullivan has been instrumental in supporting this program. Ann Morris Advertising was instrumental in seeing that *Homework Solutions for Weary Students and Their Parents* was published. Judy Fleischmann's guidance proved a spring-board for my speaking career.

Sande Hart, Emily Hart, Matthew Hart, Mary Reynolds, Carol Cherney, Lynn Bogart, Melvin Powers, Karen Hainlen, Linda Ecker, Corrie Grudin, Cindy Helliwell, Linda Abbitt, Kathy Henderson, Marci Schultz, Jackie and Greg Pensa, Tony Mercuro and Jack Canfield were great coaches and friends. Patrick Santoro's shared knowledge has taken my teaching to a different level. Anna Gollwitzer's visionary strength set an example to which I could aspire, and Marius provided pleasant periodic breaks from computer work. A special thanks goes to Mark Victor Hansen, who sent me on the path of self-publishing with what appeared to be a chance meeting several years ago on a beach in Kona. He proved to me that there are no accidents in life. This book would not have been possible without the capable direction of William Kritzberg. He helped me understand that the universe works and that you never know when an angel will appear. Teresa London took my vision and made it a reality. Her talent amazes me. Last but not least, I want to express my appreciation to the teachers, parents, and students who have eagerly shared their success stories and who encouraged me to share this program with others.

Students who know how they study best are the happiest and the learning process is fun for them.

Table of Contents

I am so excited to be sharing this program with you.

Before you begin, take a few minutes to record any questions you have about homework and any concerns you hope will be addressed in this book. If your questions have not been answered after reading this book, contact Ms. Olivadoti for assistance.

-
-
-
-
-
-
-

There are also pages provided at the back of this book for recording any "Try Its." These are ideas you want to try right away.

“If we teach our students 'how' to learn, the 'what' is easy.”

Victoria Olivadoti

“Limitations in our capacities are self-created.”

Author Unknown

Chapter 1

A New Role for Teachers

Implementing this program requires very little change on the part of the teacher, yet the results are amazing. It simply calls for teachers to redefine their roles. Thirty-five years ago I was a young teacher. I entered my first teaching assignment as a neophyte armed with all the psychology that was guaranteed to create a nurturing, thriving classroom. I was enthusiastic and excited to be teaching eleven- and twelve-year-olds. I had high aspirations for a making a difference in their lives. After all, I knew all the strategies that promised to create an effective classroom environment.

Then the students entered. I knew exactly what to say; I had rehearsed all the phrases guaranteed to command respect. However, my students did not have the benefit of having read the same material and therefore did not use the correct responses. Out the window went all the methods that I had studied so diligently. They would work to a certain extent, but they didn't elicit the responses the psychology books had promised.

It wasn't until a wiser, very kind and experienced teacher observed my angst over the lack of proper responses. She shared the following words that changed the way I approached my new profession. "Vicki, you are a very enthusiastic teacher. Keep in mind that **students are going to learn in spite of you and not learn in spite of you**. Just do your best every day and that is all you can ask of yourself."

From that moment on, I began to see the role of teacher as a motivator or salesperson of education. A new definition of educator was that of "promoter." Since students' motives for learning varied and since they held the key to whether they were going to learn or not learn, it became important to look at education from a different perspective. It was not a set of lesson plans that taught data. I placed less importance on teaching content and more importance on helping students understand their unique learning process.

As this process developed, it was necessary to look at the skills students needed to become independent learners. The students came from diverse backgrounds. Some had parents who were over involved, while other parents lacked study skills themselves. It was apparent that if the students were to succeed, they would need strategies to support them.

Using homework as the students' lab shifts our role to that of guide. When educators make this shift in the primary grades, homework takes on a different purpose. It no longer appears to be busy work. It becomes students' time to learn time management skills and an opportunity to try different learning strategies. The strategies they are asked to apply in homework quickly help them discover their own style of learning. The homework process also aids students in learning how to deal with the stress related to homework that challenges them.

The benefits of the program are varied. One that is of value to schools is the increased performance on standardized tests. When children receive help at home and then they return to school and receive assistance, they don't develop strategies for testing. Then when they are tested and have a question, the first thing teachers say to them is "I'm sorry, I can't help you." This sets off the stress response and the student won't be able to remember even the simplest concepts.

The struggle enhances long-term memory and a sense of pride is felt once the challenge is met.

Chapter 2
Attitude Survey

Take a few moments to get in touch with how the following words or phrases make you feel. What emotional response is evoked in you when you hear them?

Failure

Mistakes

Criticism

Losing Items

Perfectionism

Stress

Messy Desks

The manner in which teachers respond to students' failures and imperfections will frame the end result of our efforts. Seeing failure as an opportunity for change, mistakes as cues to show us what we don't know or changes we need to make, self-evaluation as a replacement for criticism, losing items as an indicator of a need for a system of organization, perfectionism as an indicator of a fear of failure, stress as an opportunity to teach stress reduction methods and a messy desk as an indicator that a child needs paper and time management skill training.

When homework is at an indpendent level, students have a postive experience and learn how they learn best.

Chapter 3

Value of Homework

Homework can serve many purposes:

- It allows students to test their understanding of concepts they have learned. It places time and space between new concepts and requires students to practice information recall.
- It allows students to experiment with problem-solving and study strategies to determine which approaches work best.
- It encourages focused and purposeful listening.
- It offers methods for learning time management and preplanning.
- It offers opportunities to apply study methods for varied subjects.
- It helps develop dendrite highways for retrieval of information.
- It offers opportunities to teach stress-reduction methods that transfer to test-taking situations.

- **It demonstrates to teachers what their students do not know or understand.**

- It focuses on the product to determine the effectiveness of the process.

◆

"We do not know what our students do not know until they tell us what they do not know!"

◆

Chapter 4

What Homework Should Not Be!

Homework should never be punitive. Students who have difficulty completing assignments during class are not having a positive experience and are sending us a clear message that they are avoiding the work. Sending the work home to be completed places the burden on the parents to get the work completed. They are not always the best teachers for their children. They may be knowledgeable, but the negative human emotional response that surfaces when children express frustration with their work can turn homes upside down.

It is our responsibility to assist students in determining why they are not experiencing success during class and offer strategies for turning that around. I have never a met a lazy student who did not do their homework because it was easy. There is always an underlying reason for students' failure to complete work. Sending it home is not going to achieve anything other than creating a negative attitude toward the subject that is posing challenges for these students in the first place. Regardless of why the work is not complete, to assign incomplete seatwork for homework, adding it to the homework load, is

counterproductive. When we send students home to finish incomplete work, we feed the insecurity in the parents and overwhelm students, resulting in the avoidance of the homework. For this reason, we must be sure that our homework nurtures the learning process and does not become punitive.

This book will demonstrate how to be sure the homework is at an independent level for your students and will make homework a positive experience for all students.

Learning is a choice that students make—the same choice they make when they choose to dress for school. Helping them connect with the power of their choices improves performance.

"Johnny, you made the choice to come to school with your pants on. Why didn't you come in your pajamas?"

"I'd be embarrassed."

"You can make the same choice to bring in your homework and not miss Hall of Fame."

Chapter 5

Elements of a Strong Homework Program

A well-structured homework program can encourage the development of many important skills. It promotes meaningful questioning, planning strategies and creative problem solving. It will also motivate students to become active listeners and to listen to their peers, thus learning strategies they might not have considered on their own. It forces students to become more interactive with the material. It instructs students in paper management and time management strategies. The most valuable result is the confidence students gain and the way they change their thinking about what they can accomplish on their own. To achieve these goals, the program must include the following elements:

1. All work must be at an independent level. It must not require further instruction. It must be work students can complete on their own.

2. Classroom time must be allocated for reviewing the work. This time will allow students an opportunity to review the work as if they are going to begin it right away and ask questions for clarification. This is a very powerful learning tool and will allow each student to process the information. When students ask clarifying questions, they are processing the information and therefore the answer has a better chance of becoming part of their long-term memory.

3. Classroom time must be allocated for discussion of challenges and solutions from the previous evening's homework.

4. Opportunities must exist to discuss problems faced when homework is missing and how such challenges can be resolved in the future. Group and individual counseling sessions are required and must be ongoing throughout the year.

5. Most importantly, students need a system for organization of materials, time and project planning.

6. Self-evaluation of progress on a daily, weekly and monthly basis is a must.

7. The homework program requires instruction in methods and uses of visualization for retrieval of information.

8. It must offer opportunities for students to learn how to deal with weaknesses to assure success for every child.

Chapter 6

The Vicious Cycle
Home-School Dilemma

Understanding how homework became the huge issue it is today will help us unravel the mystery and create a wonderfully enriching program for students. In the **seventies,** students were expected to complete homework independent of their parents and teachers. They submitted work in varying degrees of completion and with errors; most work was less than perfect. That was the norm. Parents were less involved and trusted the educational system. If a student was disciplined at school, there was a good chance he would also be disciplined at home. Parents expected their children to be obedient. In this framework, students were required to rely on their own resources. Though parents did help at times with the concepts, most parents expected the school to do the instruction and expected students to listen in class. Homework was not designed to accelerate education, but was a reinforcement of instruction. It was not designed to teach students how to take a test, but was an opportunity to allow students to test their understanding of concepts.

The **eighties** posed a new problem—the introduction of parent involvement in the classroom. This was a great idea in theory, but had repercussions. While it was wonderful having an extra pair of hands, it allowed the parent a new view of the classroom. From the inside, parents could see how their children measured up to the rest of the class. Parents were very competitive and not trained about what was appropriate to discuss about their classroom observations. This was painfully clear to me when I overheard some parents talking in the park one day.

Every Thursday our students had early dismissal and the mothers would meet in the park and have a gabfest while their children ate lunch and played. I was enlightened as two parents began talking about their children's second-grade classroom. The class had taken a timed test of multiplication facts.

The conversation went as follows:

"Johnny got 100% on his multiplication test today. Did your Mark study for the test last night?"

"Why do you ask?"

"Well, it appeared that he didn't do very well."

Johnny's mother had no business sharing what she observed while helping in the classroom. She had alarmed her friend needlessly. The teacher was perfectly happy with Mark's performance in class. He was a top student in science and was an avid reader. Math wasn't his strongest area. Had she been concerned about his math performance, she would have shared her concern with Mark's mother.

What occurred placed a vicious cycle in motion. Now that Mark's mother was concerned, she began nagging her son about his homework every day. "Did you do your homework? Let me check it." As she became more involved, she shared with me that Mark began making more mistakes on his homework and was requiring more of her time with instruction. She asked me to do some tutoring and I agreed. I met with his teacher and discovered her confusion over Mark's declining interest in the classroom. She told me that she was planning a parent conference to find out what had happened at home to bring about this change. The truth was that one event in the park had caused the change. Prior to his mother's involvement, Mark had paid attention in class. Math was not his strong suit, but he was making excellent progress in the subject.

Once his mother began to put pressure on him for perfection in math, he turned off. She so wanted the other parent to see Mark getting 100% on his timed tests that she became obsessed with practice. The poor boy was burned out. The result was not the positive one she desired. Parent involvement did not come with parent education. The information gleaned by a volunteer did not remain confidential and was counterproductive.

As the media began investigating our educational system, a new fear surfaced. The question about the quality of education and the effectiveness of the teachers raised more parental fear. The schools were under continual criticism and the negative result was that students were hearing their parents questioning the system. I have observed many students manipulate the situation by feeding into their parents' fears. It is not uncommon to hear a parent respond with anger when their children announce that the teacher did not teach a concept found on their homework. This happens. **In the "old days," the parent would tell the child to go back to school and ask for needed help.** But today, with heightened parental fears of failure, parents accuse teachers of not doing their job.

Once the parents feeds into the fear that their child is not going to make it because the teacher is not doing his job, they charge into action. They either do the instruction themselves or they pay a tutor to do that which the teacher would do **if he knew the student was struggling.** Many times the parents do the work for their children. If the work is corrected at home and the student is given instruction at home, the teacher is receiving incorrect information about the effectiveness of the instruction. To do a good job, the teacher needs to know that the student did not grasp the concept.

Another situation has arisen in the last few decades. Teachers are expected to get through curriculum whether students are ready for it or not. They are finding that they need to make up for lost time in class by assigning work for homework. Much of this work does require instruction. Parents who are not equipped with teaching strategies will often do the work to avoid the stress that trying to teach their own children creates. This situation also feeds into the parents' insecurity and lack of confidence with the system.

The chart on the next page depicts the vicious cycle that occurs nightly in homes nationwide and shows why parents and teachers must be aware of its existence. Our awareness will help us break this cycle. A well-structured homework program will accomplish this goal.

On a side note, I find it very interesting that we would never consider putting an unskilled teacher in the classroom, yet nightly—and without training—we ask parents to teach subjects they haven't seen since they were in school. In fact, many of the concepts their children are learning weren't even taught when they were in school. Even educators are not equipped to deal with the negative emotions connected with teaching their own children.

So how do we break this vicious cycle? It only takes a simple tweaking of your program. It might result in withdrawal for the over-involved parent, who need their own attention, but the results are amazing.

Vicious Cycle

Step 1
Teacher Assigns Homework

Step 2
Student doesn't truly understand the work. Nor does the student ask for help before class is over.

Step 3
Student complains to parents that the teacher didn't explain the assignment. Student cries or has a hissy-fit.

Step 4
Parent worries that the child will fail if no help is given. Pressure increases to give assistance.

Step 5
Student completes the work after a stress filled evening. It is completed with parental assistance. It is free of errors.

Step 6
Student turns in work done correctly.

Step 7
Teacher corrects work and moves on assuming the teaching methods used were effective.

Chapter 7

Focused Attention and Effective Questioning

Students receiving assistance on all subjects have no need to listen in class. Suzy demonstrated this in class during instruction of new material. I noticed Suzy daydreaming. "Suzy, if you don't listen carefully you will not know how to do tonight's homework." Her reply forever changed the way I teach.

"That's okay. My mom will teach me tonight."

Within moments of exposure to information, we decide whether it is important to store. If students always are helped with assignments, it is understandable that these students will have no urgency to pay attention. Since they didn't focus while the information was given, they can actually believe they never saw the concept or that the teacher never taught it.

Creating meaningful homework, at the student's independent level and restricting parent involvement or tutoring, will inspire a new sense of urgency to listen. If students must listen to complete the work in the evening without help, they will ask questions, listen to the answers and listen to their classmates' questions as well. **It works!!**

Tutoring to support students can be very helpful, but using a tutor to help with homework is counterproductive. Students need to listen to their teachers and learn to ask questions that will help them communicate what they do not know. If they rely heavily on using tutors, they never learn how to work with teachers to get their personal needs met. The tutoring creates a crutch. If students need support in an area, tutoring can be helpful and in many cases necessary, but not to do a student's homework.

The only way to know that work is at an independent level is to allow opportunities for students to look at the work as if it were to be done right away. Allowing students to ask clarifying questions will reveal their understanding of the material. If their questions indicate they are not ready for the material and that further instruction is needed, educators need to be flexible and assign something that is at their level. If an assignment appears to be difficult, asking students to work through the assignment and create questions to ask the following day will also help them listen carefully when the follow-up instruction is given. They will be seeking the answers to their own questions and consequently will listen intently.

Modeling the questioning technique may be necessary in some classrooms. If students are not good at predicting with what they may have difficulty, the teacher can pose some questions that will demonstrate how to look at the material.

There are many benefits to this method. First, students learn to look at their work differently. Second, they learn from their peers' questions. If they lack the skills necessary in the art of asking questions, they can learn from observing how their peers look at the work. When the stage is set, students listen more intently because their peers may ask a question they had not thought about, and that question might be something they will encounter at home. By removing the parent from homework involvement, students are more inclined to listen to every question asked.

Most students do not know what it means to listen. They need to be taught what listening looks like. Students can identify with playing a video game and the type of attention they give the television when focusing on the moves of the game. This is a powerful analogy in teaching students what you want from them. "I need you to pretend I am a video game and want you to give me the type of attention you would give the game. You know how to tune out all other noise when you are playing, so pretend that whatever else is happening around you in class is like your mother interrupting your video game playing and tune it out."

Elements of Focused Listening

1. The student sits on the edge of his chair with his feet flat on the floor. This puts his spine in an upright position; that has a positive effect on the vestibular system. The vestibular system, when balanced, increases one's ability to focus on information. It is helpful to share this information with students.

   New ball chairs are built in such a way that they

force students to use the proper posture for concentration. They also allow active students to gently bounce to release extra energy. Bouncing or jumping up and down prior to a period that requires deep concentration, such as test taking or instruction of a new concept, will improve student performance.

2. Leaning forward helps with concentration.
3. Forming questions as the teacher is instructing and recording those questions on scrap paper improves listening. If students hold onto questions, they are missing the instruction that follows. By recording them on paper, they are free to receive the remaining instruction, which often answers their questions.
4. Not permitting help at home with homework improves listening and questioning during class instruction tenfold!
5. Placing importance on all questions asked and the need to listen to each other's questions and answers improves listening.
6. It is important to only answer a question once. If a question is asked again, refer the student to the peer who originally asked the question. If students know you will answer every question only once, they listen more intently to others' questions and the answers you provide. (I do make an exception now and then. But if students detect a pattern of answering a question more than once, they will stop listening.)
7. Announce when you are introducing something new that requires focused attention. Listening is the hardest skill students need to learn. Today's children are very visual and most of our teaching is verbal. For this reason, students tend to tune us out. It is only fair to tell them when you want them to tune in at a high attention level.

♦

If your students are tired, focused listening will be difficult.
Emphasize the need for a good sleep routine to improve their attentivenes.

Questions are the most powerful tool for learning. When children wonder, they seek the answer and listening skills improve.

◆

Try Three and Then Ask Me!

Ask your students to try three different strategies. If they still have trouble, have them ask a question about what they don't know.

◆

Chapter 8
Trips to "LaLa Land"

"LaLa Land" is a place students go when they have lost focus. They can lose focus for a variety of reasons. Sometimes it is because we just talk too much. Other times they go there when we are discussing something that doesn't interest them. They may take a trip when they find a subject difficult and want to escape the horrible feeling of not understanding what is going on. Regardless of why they take their trips, we can help them take fewer of them by identifying what happens. We can describe how it feels to go to "LaLa Land" and how to prevent taking too many trips.

Discuss "LaLa Land" with students as follows: "LaLa Land" is a place we go to escape boredom or difficult subjects. Sometimes we end up there without even realizing it. We might find ourselves outside even though we are in the classroom. We might find ourselves at the beach or on a golf course. But one thing is true—we are not in the classroom mentally. Sometimes we will come back from a trip to "LaLa Land" and everyone in the class is doing an activity and we don't have a clue what they are doing. Have any of you ever experienced that?

"To avoid going to "LaLa Land" we need to start practicing focused attention. This is the type of attention you use when you are playing video games and can't hear your mother calling you. You sit differently. The focused student sits on the edge of his chair. Your posture will be straight and your hands will be on the desk. You will be thinking about what is being said and repeating it in your head. You might even be taking notes or doodling on a piece of paper to keep focused. It is a decision you make and if you are a trip taker, it will take real effort on your part to stay focused. If you should feel like taking a trip because you don't know what we are talking about, feel free to raise your hand and let me know. I don't know what you are not understanding until you tell me what you are not understanding. I would rather you share your frustration instead of taking a trip and missing even more important information. When you feel yourself going off, change your position or squeeze a stress ball. Try doing "hookups" (strategies from Brain Gym) to increase your attention. You can even do some chair pull-ups. Get creative. You might think of something else that will work even better.

One student recently came into class with a thick rubber band around his wrist. His father had gone to a business training session and they gave out the rubber bands with instructions to flick it and remind themselves of their goals. My student thought it would be something that would work for him. Guess what? It did! We can't discount the effectiveness of a strategy that works for a student, no matter how silly it sounds to us. When the student comes up with the idea, there is a better chance that it will be successful.

Students learn to take their trips fewer and farther between.

Chapter 9
Learning Triangle: Student, Teacher and Parent

Who should be involved in the homework program? The student, the teacher and the parent all need to be a part of a successful program. Each of their roles needs to be clearly defined.

The Students' Role

The students' role is to have total responsibility for homework. Students are not often included in the decision making about homework. They are told how, when and where to do the assignment by both their teachers and their parents. Students are very capable of taking on more responsibility when it comes to homework. The students, in my opinion, are the most important component of a successful homework program and should never be excluded from the decision-making process.

Their responsibilities involve the following:

1. Recording assignments and activities in a day planner.
2. Reviewing their personal schedule daily, including all extracurricular activities, to determine when to complete the assignment.
3. Collecting all materials needed to complete the assignment.
4. Reviewing the materials and asking questions for clarification.
5. Putting the materials in the "Incomplete Folder."
6. Taking materials home.
7. Deciding when and where to complete the work.
8. Completing the work.
9. Reviewing to be sure all work is complete.
10. Placing work in the "Completed Folder."
11. Highlighting the assignment in the day planner.
12. Placing the homework book in the backpack.
13. Returning the work promptly at the beginning of class.
14. Reviewing all graded work and identifying the cause of mistakes.
15. Making mistakes and prescribing changes that will bring different results.

For students, it is an issue of deciding. Students as young as age two decide what they are going to do and not do. Deciding to learn is one thing all students have in common, no matter what their intellectual ability. They choose either to learn or not to learn. We can be the best educators on earth, but if students have decided they don't want to learn, there is little we can do. Our goal is to motivate them to make decision changes. On the other hand, even if a student is plagued with learning differences, if he decides to learn, nothing will stand in his way. The key is getting students to see the value in pursuing goals and overcoming obstacles. For now, it is important for educators to point out to students that they do have a choice in how they perform and that making the decision to use focused attention is half the battle.

The Teacher's Role

The teacher will provide appropriate homework at the students' independent level. He will be sure to teach the necessary skills to complete the assignment. He will provide adequate time for review of the evening's assignment. If it becomes apparent that the work is too difficult to be done independently, based on students' questions, the teacher must change the assignment and administer instruction to allow for proper understanding of the material. Teachers must offer several strategies and opportunities to test understanding, free of grades.

This is difficult for many teachers due to the pressures of standardized tests. Teachers today are feeling the pressure to present a certain amount of material so their students will perform well on the tests. The irony is if we allow enough time for questions and opportunities for self-exploration, students will actually cover more material and there will be less need for reteaching concepts. That is the power of "the question."

As educators, we need to empower students with the discovery of how their choices determine results. If we use every opportunity to help students understand how their choices create results, and how changing behaviors can change results, we will empower them. We will clearly define our role for students. We will assist students in setting goals and guide students through the self-discovery process. We will provide the following instruction to guarantee success:

1. How to use a homework system.
2. Goal setting and results evaluation.
3. The skill of scheduling—hourly, daily, weekly, monthly and quarterly.
4. How to preview material.
5. Strategies for reading questions.
6. How to ask a question.

7. How to evaluate results and make any behavioral changes necessary to change the results.
8. Intrinsic and/or extrinsic guidance.
9. Specific standards that are clearly stated.
10. Learning-style information and instruction in how it applies to each student.
11. Instruction in goal setting. Define and clearly describe a successful student.

The Parent's Role

The parent's role needs to be that of facilitator, someone who guides the child in good decision making. The parent is not and should not be a teacher or tutor. Educators must retrain parents and revise their thinking about their role. The media has created a vicious cycle; to break it we need to give parents language they can use to work with us instead of against us. We need the parents to support what we are teaching and help students learn from their mistakes. Parents need education about how students learn to change behavior and make new choices based on the knowledge they gain from past mistakes.

Parents need to examine their children's schedules to be sure there is time for homework. Many students are faced with mind-blowing schedules after school. Students need time to play. If they are not given time to play at home, they will find the time to play. It will more than likely be in the classroom. Parents need to let their children struggle and encourage them to find their own solutions to challenges. Parents can give undivided attention to do something fun when children complete their work independently.

A Parent's Meeting: Taming the Homework Monster

For this program to be a success, the parents need to buy into the idea. The parent meeting provides a model for a parent information night that should be held during the first week of every school year. It will help you define the parents' role and hopefully provide your parents with strategies they can employ to support you and their children in the effective homework program.

Parents need to create an environment in which it is safe for children to take risks and suffer the consequences or the benefit of their labor. They need to provide encouragement to work through the tough times. For students to reach their potential, they need to be encouraged to be self-reliant. Parents encourage self-reliance when they let go and allow children to walk alone, ride a bike without training wheels or swim independently.

They need to encourage self-reliance in homework. Giving parents the language to do just that is why parent education is a must. If this homework program is to be totally effective and bring about powerful results parents must embrace it. *Homework Solutions; A Parent's Guide-The Missing Link Between Home and School* and *Homework Strategies for Weary Students and Their Parents* provide the language and reasoning for empowering students to become self-advocates.

An Argument for Limiting and Defining Parent Participation

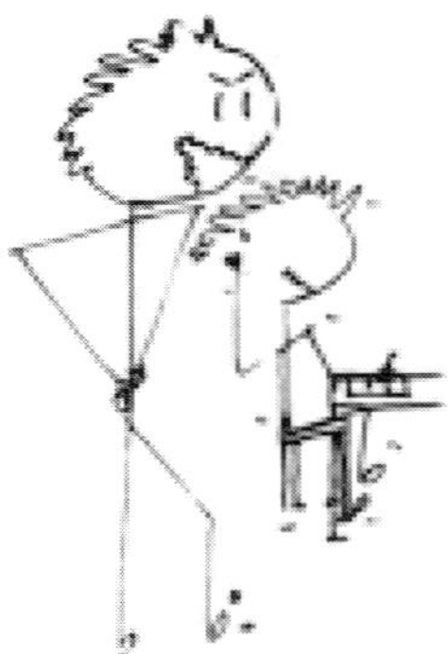

When students lack organizational skills it is possible that their parents also lack those skills. They may be professionals and because they have been successful, we may assume they understand organizational strategies, but many do not. I have worked with many bright children of successful parents. After I teach the fundamentals of organization, these achieving parents say that they wish they had learned these strategies when they were young. It would have made their climb to the top less stressful. One student announced that her very successful mother needed to learn the strategy of backward planning, because their home life was horrible because of deadlines for her jewelry catalog. For this reason, we need to teach the fundamentals and students can share them with their parents. Assuming that students know nothing about homework strategies will keep us mindful of providing organizational strategies for the nightly homework and every project we assign.

Consider the emotional response evoked when a student says, "I don't get it." It creates tension for everyone involved. Parents don't always know how to deal with this comment and dive right into teaching.

What results are comments like, "That's not how the teacher did it. You're not doing it right!" Not understanding that a new method of instruction can be even more confusing for children, the parent's response is often, "I went to college, so I know how to do this problem." Tension mounts and a shouting match often occurs. Once the homework is complete, this negative emotional response carries over into other aspects of family life.

Demystification

Organizational Challenge

Understanding disorganized students and helping them understand themselves is of key importance in this program. Demystification of the challenges faced by students who are not naturally organized will make your job much easier.

When students are faced with organizational dysfunction, the following dialogue can help them deal with their challenge: "Managing your homework is difficult for you. Do you know why? Each of our brains functions differently. Your brain sees numbers and understands them easily. Your brain, however, has a hard time making sense of where to put materials once you are finished using them. It's not your fault. It means you need to take time to be aware of what you are doing with papers and supplies, and where they need to be placed. You need to give deliberate attention to what you are doing.

It's not easy, but it will become second nature the more you practice. It's just like learning how to kick the ball in soccer. Did you kick the ball into the net the first time you tried? No, you had to practice the skill over and over before it became natural. The same is true with organizing your papers.

I am going to provide you with a system for being successful. It has helped many students whose brains work just like yours. You will need to give it the same concentration and practice time you give to your soccer practice. In the beginning, you must ask yourself, "What do I need to do with this paper?" The more you practice this skill, the more natural it will become. Your disorganization may never disappear, but you can be successful with this program. Every student like you who has practiced this process has been successful. You can too! You have to be willing to make mistakes and learn from them. Are you up for the task? Great! That's 90% of the solution and the place to start on your road to success."

Students struggle with paper management dysfunction, which can create tremendous stress, until they are taught a process for managing their papers.

Chapter 10
When to Start?

When should we begin independent homework? The sooner we introduce homework, the easier it will be to create independent students. The best time to do so is when students are young. Beginning in kindergarten, students are ready to take on some responsibilities and in most cases are very eager to do so. They are capable of asking parents to let them read aloud and take responsibility for managing their assignments. They are closer to the ground. They can fall, pick themselves up, brush themselves off and try again. If one looks at falls as opportunities and not disasters, they offer students wonderful opportunities to see what does and does not work.

If we leave the training wheels on the bike, our children will be riding to high school on three wheelers. Of course, peer pressure would encourage the children to ask their parents to remove the training wheels. When we introduce a program of independence the children embrace it and their peers will follow.

The best time to introduce homework is on the first day of school. Kindergartners have been waiting for this day since they can remember. They want to read, they want to do math and they want to do homework. We must seize the moment and begin our homework training immediately, before they form bad habits. Starting with an assignment every night that is to be returned the next day establishes a pattern for children. Kindergartners can be taught to take a paper and place it in the left-hand side of a folder, take it home, complete it, put it in the right-hand side of the folder and return the work the next day.

A suggested curriculum is available online at www.homeworkdoc.com.

Power Struggles Occur When Students Feel Powerless!

♦

90% of all homework challenges can be overcome when students are put in control.

Chapter 11
The How
A Model

The how of the homework program is multi faceted. It is deliberate in part and yet largely determined by the errors students make. Though elements of the program are constant, they are never the same year to year. Instead, they are based upon what students bring with them each year.

We become coaches and homework facilitators. After we instruct students in a process that guarantees success, we must monitor their progress by evaluating their successes and failures and demystifying why they were successful and why they experienced a setback. Then our role is to help students develop strategies to avoid any further setbacks. Most students embrace the process immediately. Roughly 10% of the student population will have minor setbacks; 1% will struggle through many counseling sessions until they find the strategies that work for them. I have not met a student who did not eventually experience success.

One crucial aspect of this program is that it requires a nurturing environment. As educators, we say one thing and yet give students a different impression based upon our responses. We often hear teachers say, "There is no such thing as a stupid question." Yet a teacher's facial expression can give students a different message. For this reason, we need to set the stage for understanding teachers' responses so students feel comfortable asking questions and making mistakes.

A Model: The First Day

The first thing we must do is to clarify for students why we come to school. Some students come to school because they love learning. Others come to school because they love to be with their friends; for them, recess is the highlight of their day. Whatever their motivation, we need to determine it from the beginning. Each student shares what he wants to accomplish by the end of the year. It is important to establish a feeling of community and accept all answers. I even share that my reason for going to school was to talk with people, since I love to do it so much. We have to appear human with faults and share with students, so they don't get the impression that we expect perfection. I also share that I was not good at math or reading when I was young and that those subjects were hard for me.

Allowing students to choose their seats in the class establishes the concept that they are in control and capable of making decisions for themselves. They need the opportunity to make choices within the parameters of well-established standards of performance.

I have been asked what I say to establish an environment that promotes self-discovery. The following is what I say to my students on the first day of school:

"I know that your first choice might be to sit next to your best friend—that would have been mine. But as you make the decision about where to sit, I want you to consider what type of learner you are. Keep in mind your purpose for being here. If you are the type of learner who is more inclined to talk, like me, then you might choose to sit by yourself, so you will not be tempted to talk during work time. You can save that for recess instead of spending recess doing your class work, which is what happens if you do not use your time wisely. You may need to sit right in the front, so you are forced to pay attention. You may want to sit at the very back, so you are free to move around a little without disturbing your classmates. You may also choose to sit in the back if you find it easier to do your work standing up. If too much activity distracts you, you might find the perimeter of the classroom a better place.

"When you decide where you will sit, consider if you need to be by yourself or if you can sit next to someone you know. If you choose to sit next to someone you know, you may remain there until I see that you are not being productive. As long as you are doing your job, you will be able to remain in the seat you choose. As you make your choice, consider that your choice of seat must be one that allows you to listen carefully, complete work in a timely fashion and does not create a distraction for any other student. Consider whom you will sit next to, in front of and behind. If you do not get your choice of seat, let me know and we will work something out." The children choose their seats and class begins.

Most students want to sit next to a friend. The following instruction gives students another option that will not offend the friend and nurtures good learning choices:

"A huge responsibility goes along with sitting next to a friend. If you feel you can handle the responsibility, I will give it to you. If sitting next to a friend is not going to work for you, there is nothing wrong in telling a friend that you like him, but you are afraid you might talk too much, so you are going to choose not to sit next to each other. Your friend will understand and you can use your recess to chat."

I proceed to allow students to make their choices. This sets the stage for the discussion of choices and the consequences of actions. Students naturally stay away from those who would bother them. They will also choose not to sit next to a friend and it is now acceptable to do so. It is amazing how responsible their choices are when they are making them and not the teacher.

Janelle approached me and said, "Ms. O, I don't think my seat is in a good place for me. May I move to the front of the room?" It is ironic that many of my students have come to the same realization. I just don't have a room wide enough to accommodate their desires. It is interesting that extroverts often choose to sit in the center of the classroom surrounded by many students, while introverts choose the perimeter of the classroom.

Of course, there are always those students who talk too much and they are often moved the first day. This lets the other students see that their decision-making is valued, but that they have to abide by the rules or they will lose the privilege. Later they are allowed to try it again to see if they are ready for the responsibility. Once they regain the privilege, they rarely abuse it.

The stage is now set for the first step in an effective homework program. **Confidence is the key**. The confidence in students' ability to be independent and the confidence they will gain as a result of this program is what makes the program work. My confidence in their ability to be successful no matter the odds is 90% of the reason this program works. They are given a tried and true system that guarantees success and helps them build confidence in themselves to meet any challenge.

Students value our faith in their ability to do what is in their own best interest. They rarely disappoint themselves or me. Once we have established this foundation, it is time to introduce the homework program. Though I introduce this concept in third grade, I have also used this same approach in every grade I have taught. The words are slightly changed, but the essence remains.

Using a day planner is a very grown-up responsibility. Presenting it as such will make your students feel important. The following has been very successful:

"Now that you are in third grade, you are ready to become independent students. You do not need any help with homework because you are grown up now."

This comment usually creates great deal of fear in students. They have become so dependent on their parents for help that they don't believe they can do it themselves. Reassure them by saying, "I know you think you need help with your homework, but I am going to ask you to do me a huge favor. I'm going to ask you to keep your homework a private activity. Your parents have a job they do, I have a job I do and homework is going to be the job that you do—completely by yourself. I don't even want you to ask them about a word or question that doesn't make sense.

"There is a very important reason I need you to avoid getting any help from your parents. Homework is an opportunity for me to see if I have done a good job. If you get help at home, then I will think I am teaching you the way you learn best. If you have trouble with homework and you come in the next day and share it with me, then I will learn how to do a better job for you. I also want you to learn how you learn best. I can tell a great deal about what you do and do not know by the mistakes you make. Your mistakes are the best learning tool for me and for you. So to help me be the best I can be, I need you to do your very best on your homework. Not your parents' very best, but your very best, and that will be good enough for me. In this way, we both can become the best we can be."

"I also want to assure you that if you are doing your very best and you make mistakes, you will not be punished. We can learn more from our mistakes than we can when we do something perfectly. I am concerned with the type of mistakes you make, not that you are making them. Mistakes are one of the most important tools we have as teachers. They tell us what you don't know."

The next step is to introduce the homework notebook and how to use it. This approach is multi sensory. For students to be motivated to use this system, they also need to see the reasoning for each part of it. Giving purpose to each step will motivate students to do them.

To help create intrinsic reward extrinsic motivators are helpful in the beginning. "Hall of Fame" is a possible reward for students who complete all steps of the homework process daily. On Friday, students who turned in homework daily and highlighted their agendas receive fifteen minutes of free play. Those fifteen minutes help us accomplish more in the week than one can imagine. It also gives us time to counsel students who have encountered a challenge. Missing Hall of Fame provides students with motivation to change the behavior that is not working. It is also a weekly monitoring device. When we discuss counseling students, we will cover the procedures for those missing Hall of Fame. Whatever your reward system, use it to give constant reinforcement of each step.

"Homework is more than an activity; it is a system. I created this system for students whose desks looks like they threw up and for students who have trouble managing their time. The first part of your homework system is this three-ring binder. It has a pocket in the front and a pocket in the back. Use your permanent marker to label each part. I would like you to write the word 'Incomplete' on the front pocket. Now I would like you to write the word 'Complete' on the back pocket. Why do you think I have asked you to label these pockets in this manner?"

Listen to all responses, showing respect to each student. Ask students to label the pockets, because labeling prevents them from putting papers in the wrong place. (My assistant decided to label the shelves of my storage closet. I jokingly told her that she was a very optimistic person, thinking that I could adhere to the labels. However, when I put away the stapler, I could not place it on the shelf labeled "pins." The same thing happens to students.)

"In the front pocket, you will place the work that needs to be completed as homework. Once it is completed, you will place it in the back pocket. These pockets will help you keep track of your homework worksheets and you will always know where your homework can be found. You will not have to rummage through your backpack looking for it.

"Will there be any work left in the front pocket when you go to bed? How will you know? When do you think would be a good time to check your notebook to be sure that all the work is complete?" (A student answers.) "I recommend not later than 7:00 p.m. In this way, you will have time to complete it if you find you forgot to do something."

The next step is to hand out the agendas. "This is going to be your most valuable tool. Take a few minutes to look carefully at it. I want you to tell me what you notice." Give students ten to fifteen minutes to look at the book. They usually experience all sorts of distractions. It is best to give students time to look at it and share what they found interesting. Once that is out of the way, you will be able to get their full attention.

"Now I would like you to take this agenda and place it in the rings. Every day you come to school there will be a homework assignment written on the board. Your job is to record that assignment in your agenda under the correct date. It is also your job to think about what you will need to complete the assignment and be sure to put that in your homework notebook. If the assignment calls for a worksheet, it is your responsibility to ask for it. I will not automatically hand it out. **You must ask for the materials.** To do your job at homework, you must leave the classroom with the materials you need, because once you leave, you will not be allowed to return to get anything. The only time you will be allowed back into the classroom will be the next morning. What does that mean you need to do?" (They will respond that they must not leave the class without checking to see that they have everything.)

"Your goal, in third grade, is to work to achieve the #1 rating. The policy in third grade is that the teachers will assist you until you demonstrate competency which gives you a rating of #2. To be #1 means you will record your assignments daily without being reminded, you will get the materials you need without prompting and you will do your homework, highlight and return your homework without reminders. I will check your day planners every day until it is clear that you are doing your job. Once you have done the steps consistently without adult help you will have earned the #1 rating."

Students who reach a competency that does not require regular checking earn the #1 rating. Those students who need teacher support earn the #2 status. In the beginning, everyone will be #2s until they learn the system. By October, most students reach the #1 status, with random checks by the teacher. If the teacher determines during the random checks that students are not following the steps, they revert to the #2 status.

"Now I will demonstrate how to properly record in and use your agendas so you can reach the #1 status. Open your agendas to September 10. You will find lines on which you are to write. Do not write too big because you may need to add assignments as the day goes on. Now record the assignment you see on the board. Do not use any abbreviations. Be very detailed in your recording, because you may have forgotten what the assignment was about when you get home. Don't rely on your memory.

If there is no homework on the board, you must ask. Do not assume there isn't any homework. Plan for homework every night, unless I say otherwise. To be sure you don't miss anything, ASK!!

"The next step is very important. You need to look at the work as if you are going to sit down right now and do it. Read each question. Determine if you understand the work. **Since I don't know what you don't know until you tell me what you don't know, I will rely very heavily on your questions.** When you have questions about the homework, record them on a sticky note. When everyone has had an opportunity to look at the sheet, I will answer all questions until everyone feels confident that they can do the work independently.

"Remember, to help me do my job you must not ask for help from your parents, no matter what. Do I have your promise? Do not worry if you make some mistakes. Remember that those mistakes help me do a better job."

The session continues with a series of questions. There are specific rules for the questions. Students must listen to their peers' questions and the answers to their questions. They may not ask the same question another student has asked. If they are still unclear, they may continue to ask questions, but ask it in a different way than their peers. As they ask questions, students offer possible solutions for resolving the challenges posed by the homework.

For example, one of the assignments called for students to find the synonym for each of their spelling words. When they reviewed the assignment, the majority of students did not know the definition of "synonym." The inclination of most teachers is to jump into a lesson on synonyms. My approach is as follows: "If you were at home and you did not have someone to tell you the definition of 'synonym,' what could you do to help yourself?" The answers vary, but the first one is usually "Look it up in the dictionary." Accept all answers and continue. "What if you didn't have a dictionary at home? Since homework is practice for test taking and you can't use a dictionary or the internet during a test or ask the teacher what to do, what else can you do?" There is usually dead silence, so I ask students to think about a way to solve this problem and record it on a sticky note. This is a wonderful tool to get 100% participation in the thinking process and also stimulate the discussion, since some students simply need a few minutes to allow the creative juices to flow.

Often, students who sit passively while others provide quick responses offer the most creative answers. Because they have been so conditioned to give immediate responses, many students don't know they have the ability to find their own solutions. They immediately jump up and announce, "I don't get it," before they have given themselves a chance to think.

This "think time" demonstrates to students that not all problems can be solved immediately and sometimes your brain requires time to create. This is a strategy they can use at home instead of running to their parents the first time they encounter a challenge. The more time devoted to this process in the beginning of the school year, the more creative the students become.

Some third graders have expressed how frustrating this program was in the beginning and that they were angry with me because they lacked confidence. Once they got the hang of creative thinking, they were glad I didn't give in. They will come up with solutions to challenges that I had never thought of in my thirty years of teaching.

What is even more exciting is they learn from each other and develop a storehouse of solutions. We share all the ways they could solve this challenge. Given time to think about what a synonym might be, Kevin raised his hand and asked, "Does synonym mean the same?" I asked him why he asked that. His response was "I looked at the words in the list and the words in the problem and they looked like they meant the same thing." I could then validate his thinking. What he did was use deductive reasoning to solve that challenge.

The rest of the class heard his explanation and learned a new strategy from a peer. Because he used deductive reasoning, I won't have to reteach that concept to him. He needed the time to make that connection. The class realized that they didn't need anyone to tell them the answer and that they didn't even need a dictionary. They also learned a skill they can apply during test taking.

Preplan possible solutions to challenges students might not find the answer to during the course of doing their homework. "What if you tried all those solutions and you still couldn't figure out the answer? What could you do?" I am working toward students understanding that they can leave the question blank and ask for help the next day. They can also try their hand at the question with the risk that it be wrong. They are also welcome to come to school early the next day to get personal help.

"Where should you place this work now that you are prepared to do it this evening? That's right, you will place it in the pocket marked 'Incomplete Work.'"

Teach Visualization

Visualization is a powerful skill many students are not aware they possess. Before students can complete the next step, they need to be aware that they know how to visualize. Ask them to close their eyes and see themselves riding their bikes down the street. If they can't see it, ask if they can feel it. They may not see an actual picture, but can sense the experience. Once they identify their ability to visualize, sending them on a visual trip through a successful night of homework will assure a successful first experience.

The brain cannot tell the difference between visualization and actually doing the task. Basketball players practice visualization of making perfect shots to develop memory of making baskets. When they practice on the court, their performance is improved markedly. Using the same principle, students can visualize going through each step to assure success when they are asked to complete the first night's homework.

It is important to involve all the senses in learning the homework process. Students close their eyes and do a little preplanning. My script goes as follows:

"See yourself entering the classroom and sitting down at your desk. Can you see yourself doing that? See yourself taking out your agenda, looking at the board for the assignment and recording it. Can you see that?" (Wait for recognition by students.)

"Now see yourself asking for any worksheets you may need. Take out books that have been assigned. Take a look at the worksheet or assignment to be sure you understand every question or activity. Look at it as if you are going to do it right away. Highlight all key words. Ask questions so you know how to do your homework. Now that you understand the homework, see yourself placing the work in the 'Incomplete' pocket of your day planner. Make sure you have all the supplies you need, including glue, rulers, colored pencils, etc. Now see yourself placing your day planner in your backpack and taking it to your carpool. Do you see yourself doing these activities?

"Now you are at home. Find yourself a study place and take out your day planner and open it to today's date. You can see yourself looking at the assignments and deciding which assignment is going to be the most difficult. Label that number one. Number the rest of the assignments from the hardest to the easiest. Take out only assignment number one and do it immediately. Never have more than one assignment at your workspace at a time. Once you have completed the assignment, reread the questions and make sure you have done what the questions asked. Then place it in the 'Completed Folder.' Highlight the assignment to indicate that it is complete and ready to turn in the first thing in the morning.

"Now you will look at any other assignments and follow the same pattern for those assignments. Next, see yourself having completed all your work, having placed it in the 'Completed Folder' and having highlighted it and placed the notebook in your book bag. Now see yourself putting your book bag near the door from which you will leave the next morning. Now you will see yourself awakening, and when you are ready to go to school, you can see yourself collecting your book bag and carrying it with you to the car. You can see yourself bringing the book bag to class and taking the assignment out of the day planner notebook and placing it in the homework box.

"Now that you have completed the homework independently, how do you feel about yourself? Feel the sense of accomplishment and pride for a job done well. Take a deep breath and feel the joy of knowing that you are one day closer to going to Hall of Fame. Open your eyes. Now you can raise your hand high in the air and bend your arm at the elbow. Pat yourself on the back, because you have successfully completed your responsibility as an independent student."

The visualization of the successful pattern will fool the brain into thinking that it has already completed the pattern. Students are also having the pattern modeled without you having to be with them. This process allows you to focus students on the important behavior you want them to demonstrate and practice the motor planning of a successful day, which is essential for children who lack motor planning skills.

Students stand arm's length apart. They raise their left arms to the left and say, "Incomplete." Then they raise their right arms to the right and say, "Complete." With a swoosh of their right arms, they say, "Highlight it off." Repeat this process several times and at different times of the day.

To help them understand how to listen, give students a lesson on the art of listening. They need to have this defined for them as in Chapter 7. The best way to successfully identify the elements of listening is to connect them with something they know well. They understand the intensity of concentration when they are playing a video game. We'll call this type of attention "focused attention." They can be so focused that they can tune everything out, including the sound of their mother's voice asking them to take out the trash. They love this example.

The listener sits on the edge of his chair and gives the teacher focused attention. Focused attention is deliberate and tunes out any distractions. Even the most distractable student can practice focused attention for a period of time, especially if he knows the time involved and if he has a purpose for listening. This homework program helps improve students' attention spans. They learn what focused attention feels like and can practice it when necessary. Once they understand focused attention, alerting them to use it when a new concept is being introduced results in less reteaching.

Begin on the first day by creating potential problems. Deliberately assign a worksheet they must obtain to be successful. Do not hand it out; wait until one sharp student asks for it. Then hand the paper to just that student. More students will raise their hands and ask for the paper. There may even be a student or two who do not ask for the worksheet. Allow them to fail. It makes for a great second-day lesson. If everyone asks for the worksheet, make a point of complimenting the first student to ask.

"Aren't you glad Nancy asked for the worksheet? Had she not, many of you might have missed the first Hall of Fame. Let's thank her for showing responsibility." Students begin to share that they are behaving independently and responsibly. They love to report how they demonstrated those qualities. This encourages more of the same behavior. Peer pressure to be independent is inherent in this program.

Day Two

Once the homework is completed and returned, time needs to be allotted to discuss the strategies they employed to complete the activity. This time allows students to observe how their peers tackled the same problems in different ways. Many times, students discover that they did not ask enough questions before leaving class. Other students learn they need to pay closer attention to the questions asked and the key words in the questions. They learn from their peers. The greatest benefit is when students arrive with questions they want answered and a desire to hear how the challenge was met. They also can't wait to share how they solved the challenge. This encourages students to work at the challenge a little longer. Consequently, they listen more intently and actively participate. This results in retention of more information and less need to reteach concepts.

A benefit of this program is that students build a storehouse of strategies they can use with future challenges. They will face many of these challenges in test-taking situations. Because they have worked through the challenges in a less stressful environment, students will be more relaxed during tests and consequently, their performance will show marked improvement.

The following day begins the critical part of a successful homework program. After the class settles down, we come together to discuss the previous night's assignment. We open with a discussion of challenges faced. We begin with number one and go through each problem. At this time it is important to introduce the use of the green pen. The green pen is what I refer to as the "learning pen."

Students are expected to correct their own work and clarify why they made errors. This portion of the homework assignment is as important as doing the assignment in the first place. Far too many programs do not allow time for this process.

We use this deprogramming period to learn strategies that will assist students with their next homework assignment. As we work through each question, we discuss how students solved challenges. The solutions vary and demonstrate there is more than one way to solve a problem. It is also an opportunity to add new skills. Since the students have dealt with the challenge, they listen very carefully. Because they are rewarded for their efforts, students feel very comfortable sharing their challenges. The beauty of this process is that students who had no independent strategies leave the classroom with a storehouse of strategies. Those who had a few independent strategies leave with more.

Why does this approach work so effectively and how does it encourage students to listen carefully? It is very simple. Students looking for answers are more inclined to pay close attention to the answer. When encouraged to ask questions about the homework assignment, they are preparing their brains to seek the answer. Many times, students are able to solve problems simply by asking questions. It's amazing to see their minds jump into gear and the enlightenment shine on their faces. Those questions also save hours of reteaching. It is truly a powerful tool.

Inevitably, students will forget to do an assignment or not remember how to do the work once they attempt it at home. Since they are not used to making mistakes and are accustomed to having their parents monitor them and manage their work, the first mistakes seem huge. Initially, students share their stories accompanied by tears.

Johnny's story is an example of many that occur each year. He arrived at school a little early and asked to speak with me. He had red eyes, so I could tell he had been crying. He promptly shared how he forgot to take the paper that was assigned and when he got home it wasn't in his agenda. Since other students are going to make the same mistake at one time or another, I tried to convince him to share this first challenge with the class. His response was pretty typical.

"No."

"If I don't tell the class who made the mistake, may I still share the challenge you had so the class can learn from your mistake?"

"Sure."

"Great! I know the class will be grateful to you. Don't be too hard on yourself. This is a new responsibility to do all on your own. Will you remember to take the papers from now on?"

An interesting phenomenon occurred when I began to share Johnny's challenge.

"Class, you are really lucky today, because one of your classmates made a valuable mistake that you can all learn from. The student said I could share this experience, so you can avoid it. It was very upsetting to this student, which is how I believe you would have felt had it been you. Yesterday, this student forgot to take the worksheet. When this student got home, it was not in the agenda and therefore could not be done last night. Is there anything this student could have done when it was discovered the assignment was missing?"

The students brainstormed and came up with some very creative solutions. One solution was to come in early and do the work before school started. After we discussed the solutions, I asked the class, "Are you glad this student made the mistake? Everyone in the class agreed that they had learned a lot from this mistake. "I regret that the student did not want to share this mistake, because it helped so many other students from repeating it, or at least it taught them to know what to do if it happens to them."

No sooner had I finished the statement than Johnny raised his hand and said, " Okay, okay, it was me."

"Let's thank Johnny for making this mistake."

The entire class applauded. Johnny felt so proud. During the rest of the school year, many more students made mistakes from which the rest of the class learned strategies. Yet rather than being embarrassed, they were proud to share their challenges.

For one year, I recorded every challenge students encountered with homework and projects and the solutions they used to solve them. We turned it into ***Homework Solutions for Weary Students and Their Parents***.

Chapter 12

Why Have Homework? A Dendrite Builder

There is much controversy over the value of homework. To fully understand its value we have only to look at the function of a few of the brain's structures and systems. When we look at some basic functions of its structures, we see the value of homework. When we share this information with our students, they also see the value in doing regular homework and studying a little every night.

When students are introduced to a concept, they are using their working memories to process and understand it. They receive information through their senses. They decide within a few seconds whether the information will be used and needs to be stored. If not, it is labeled as "unnecessary to store" and dumped into what can be compared to a computer's "trash."

While students are working with a new concept, they are making connections with previously learned material and deciding whether to give it enough attention to be stored in their long-term memory for later use. It is entirely possible for students to understand a concept in class and feel they know the information, but when they try to apply the concepts later in the day, they find the information is non retrievable.

For students, I equate the working memory with the desktop of the computer. While you are typing and working on a project it is easy to see. On the other hand, the long-term memory can be compared to your computer's hard drive where you store files. Should you save a file but fail to look at it for a few weeks, it may be difficult to find.

If students don't focus enough on what they are learning, or if they do not feel an urgency to remember the information, there is a good chance they will not be able to retrieve it in the evening. They are even less likely to remember new concepts if they know they will receive assistance when they get home. The more exposure they have to a concept, the easier it will be to retrieve it at a later date.

Consider that file you saved today. If you open it only once and don't look at it for a month, you would likely have difficulty retrieving the information. If you open the file once a day for five days, there is a very good chance that in a month you would be able to retrieve the file.

The same is true for students learning new concepts. Regular practice is imperative for memory retention and retrieval. Mastery does not come with one exposure. We are exposed to a concept, we try to apply it, and attach it to something we already know, thereby increasing and strengthening connections to enable us to retrieve the information later. If we can not build a strong enough connection, it is possible that we will not be able to retrieve that information an hour later.

Dendrites aid in the transmission of information from one neuron to another in the brain. As students are exposed to new ideas, they are building dendrites and making stronger neural connections to information. Each time they work with a concept, students are building stronger passageways on which information can travel. Homework is what I refer to as the highway builders.

The following analogy assists students in recognizing the value of regular practice. Imagine you are clearing a path in the jungle. Is it hard? Just like clearing a path, learning a new concept can be difficult at first. What happens every time you go over the path? It's obvious that you prevent weeds from growing. What will happen if you do not go over the path for a few days? Of course, the weeds will grow back and if enough time elapses, the path will disappear. In much the same way, when we learn a new concept, it is difficult. Each time we interact with the concept through daily homework, the path becomes clearer. However, if we don't review the material on a regular basis, the pathway is blocked and we have difficulty retrieving the information.

Using this new information, students who are tested on a semester of work see the value of making note cards for a unit and reviewing them once a week during the semester. By doing so, they are creating superhighways to the information and keeping their paths free of weeds. When using this analogy with students, they quickly identify what happens when we come back from break and take a timed test on basic facts. It is not uncommon for students to claim that weeds grew over their paths while on vacation. The same is true of concepts that are taught in school. Though a concept was taught in second grade, it may need to be retaught in third grade, simply because too much time has elapsed and students did not have enough practice over that long period.

Try writing your name with your eyes closed. Take a minute for this experiment. Did you find it easy to do? Compare your writing to sighted writing. Is there a difference? When students are asked to do this experiment, they are surprised to find that they could not only write their names, but the writing was exemplary. When asked why they were successful, they state that because they have written it so many times, they were able to do it with their eyes closed. This offers a perfect argument for regular practice and a demonstration of how neural paths are strengthened with several exposures.

Since the passage of information along the neurons is electrical in nature, **keeping the brain hydrated is very important**.

Chapter 13

Settling the Stress Response

There are several structures in the brain that can affect student performance. One of these structures is the amygdala. Its main function is to process fear. When the body senses fear, it sets off a chain reaction that can numb the senses and block memory. It prepares the body to flight or flee a stressful situation. The problem is that it senses the tension created in the body from fear, but it does not know whether the fear is resulting from the risk of bodily harm or from the fear of failure. It makes sense that students, thinking they should know a concept, can become "brain dead" when they are faced with a homework problem they find challenging.

Since parents want to help alleviate pain for their children, they often read the problem and give their children the answer. This prevents students from discovering how to settle the amygdala and activate inhibitory pathways that decrease their response to this stress. By consciously reasoning that the stress is not serious, they cause another area of the brain to decrease the symptoms of stress, such as increased heart rate and blood pressure. This set of structures, which regulates the amount of arousal in the body, is called the Reticular Activating System (or RAS). When the amydgala is activated, the RAS increases arousal, so that the body can react to stress. This activaton, if too high, can also cause problems with concentration and can inhibit memory storage or re-trieval.

The stress response (or SR) can be conscious or subconscious. It causes the body to emit stress hormones that also interfere with retrieveal. The goal of homework is to practice reducing the stress and change the brain's chemistry to allow for retrieval. When students relax and have confidence that they are going to find the information, this chemical change occurs and clears the path for retrieval. It may find the information visually by retrieving a picture of the concept, or it may recall what was said relating to the concept.

Homework provides an opportunity for students to practice settling the amygdala, the SR and the RAS. The strategies they use to do this will later assist them during test-taking situations when they feel stressed and have difficulty retrieving information. **The goal of homework is to help students build strong neural paths, dendrite connections and teach them how to settle the amygdala, the SR and the RAS.**

If we explain it physiologically, students as young as eight years old are able to understand what happens to their bodies when they feel frustration. To effectively deal with their responses to stress, we can support students by sharing different methods to settle it. Deep breathing techniques, simple exercises and other problem-solving strategies will are very effective. Comparing the stress response to elevator doors makes sense to them. "Have you ever tried to open an elevator door once it has closed? What do you do? Wait for the next one." When students recognize that accessing information is as easy as waiting for another elevator, they can relax and allow their brain to do its job. When they feel stressed, if they relax and skip a problem with the attitude that the information will come to them, they will quickly see how the forgotten information will pop into their heads.

Begin each learning session with breathing exercises to help students relax. As they work through challenges, remind them to stretch or breathe to help them work through challenges. Before each test, remind them to breathe deeply and if they start feeling insecure, continue the breathing.

The hippocampus in the brain is comparable to the search engine of your computer. If you want to find information on the internet, the more specific question you enter, the more quickly the information appears. Your brain works the same way. The best way to activate the hippocampus memory system is through questions.

To improve reading comprehension, it makes sense to read the questions to be answered before reading the material. In doing so, we are alerting the brain to look for information and consequently comprehension will improve. If no questions are provided, creating one's own questions prior to reading will bring about the same result. The more effectively students ask questions to find information, the faster they will retrieve the answers and the stronger the neural connection will be to the concept. If an assignment is hard, students can be asked to create questions that will help them understand the concept. The more effectively we train our students to ask lots of questions about what they are learning or about what they will be doing for their homework, the more effectively they will be able to retrieve information and remember directions. When they ask the questions, they are readying their brains for the answers.

When students forget how to apply a concept in the evening, they return to class the next day armed with questions about the concept. The asking of those questions will result in improved performance by students. When they ask questions, they actively listen to the answers.

The brain has as a filter to allow for new information or to block it. It is one way to protect us from sensory overload. The filter is affected by their attitude. If students are resistant to learning a specific subject, the message they send the brain is, "Shut down, this information is unimportant." The brain does not have an infinite capacity to store information. It is continually pruning dendrites to make more room for other neural connections. We can't add more memory as we can with a computer, so the brain has to determine very quickly if the information is important enough to store. When students use negative words to describe the learning process, they retard their growth. Simply making an attitude shift will engage the hippocampus.

My students often hear me say, "Fake it until you make it." If they pretend to enjoy a subject or feed themselves positive self talk about it, it will help them use their brains more effectively. Simply saying, "I will be so happy when I find this information and then I will be able to go out and play" can help. Simply changing the internal language will improve their performance.

If students have a negative attitude toward their teachers, their ability to store and retrieve information will be affected. Students aren't required to like every one of their teachers, but if they focus on how much they hate a teacher and what a poor job the teacher is doing, they will lose an opportunity to learn. Every teacher has something to offer, even if it is merely an opportunity to learn how to "fake it until you make it." The poorest teachers were the best at educating my students in how to deal with contrary people and still get their needs met. Simply changing one's thinking from "I hate this teacher" to "I'm sure there is something I can learn from this teacher" will improve your students' performance.

An optimistic attitude will improve memory and problem solving performance. How many times have you heard stories of people who achieved greatness against insurmountable odds? Their attitude is what made the difference. The boy with no feet learned how to ride a skate-board. The girl with one arm won a surfing competition. The dyslexic student learned to read through sheer determination. She didn't know she was dyslexic until she was studying to be a teacher and learned the characteristics of dyslexia in a special needs class. There are millions of stories with the same theme: Determination and a Positive Can Do Attitude Can Create Miracles.

All that is required is that students believe what they want to do is possible and that one's past does not determine the future. Students need the support of those around them who believe that change is possible. They also need to believe it for themselves. We can tell them, but unless they believe it, no change will occur. Students choose to learn or not to learn. Their choices affect how well their brain will work.

In summary, two elements help students use the mempry and retrieval system effectively. The first is good questions. The second is a positive attitude, a belief that all things are possible for them.

Your brain's short-term memory is like the desktop of your

computer. Should you create a letter and save it, you are sending that letter to a filing system in the hard drive. The hard drive is equivalent to your brain's long-term memory. If you were to save a file and not open it for a month, you would have a hard time finding it. If you were to open that file once every other day for several days you would have no problem retrieving it in a month. Our brains are the same. If your students work with information during class and then apply the information the same evening, they are simulating the opening and closing of the file. They are also learning how to retrieve information by applying strategies. Each time they retrieve this information, they are building stronger neural paths.

If students can't retrieve a concept in the evening, it is possible that not enough neurons were activated to create a good connection. If too much time is placed between the time something is taught and the time it is applied, the brain determines that the dendrites on those neurons are not necessary to store and they prune them. This explains why students could appear to have mastered the concepts in June and have forgotten them by time they return to school in September.

For example, after a lesson in division, I assigned ten problems to complete at home. The students appeared to know the process well enough to test their understanding with homework. The following day, we discussed the evening's challenges. One girl announced that she felt she understood the material when she left class, yet when she arrived home and attempted the work, she was stumped. She tried visualizing the assignment being done on the board. She took a mental trip back to the class to try to retrieve a picture of the steps she needed to follow. She commented, "Ms. O, I tried doing the assignment last night, but when I visualized you teaching the division problem, your head was in front of the part I couldn't remember." Though she could not find the information she was looking for, she at least had a strategy to solve it. She also needed more experience with the information, before she could store it in a way that would make it easily retrieved. Another lesson she learned was to hyper focus on what was on the board when she had a clear view of it. When she returned to class, she clearly knew what she didn't know and could focus on that one step. I didn't waste time going over the previous steps, because it was clear that she understood them. She quickly grasped the concept, because she knew what she needed to learn. She listened intently and formed a new visual of the concept that she could rely on to assist her should she forget the steps by time she tried to do her homework later that evening.

Homework helps students discover if they understand information well enough to store it for future use. If students understand information at the working memory level only and have not successfully stored it in their long-term memory, they can believe they understand the concept, yet will have difficulty at home when they try to apply what they have learned. By explaining how the brain stores information and that students can think they understand something in class and later not be able to retrieve it because of lack of exposure, you will relieve your students' stress and they will have a better chance of retrieving the information later.

When students struggle with a concept at night, the next day they will be ready to receive information in a different fashion. Their focus will be more directed and learning will be solidified. They will have activated their brains and will be ready to receive. By encouraging students to return to class with questions, the learning time will be shortened, the neural connection will be strengthened and dendrites will grow connected to the concept. Their brains will be alerted to listen to the answer.

What can your students do when they have read a problem and it does not make a bit of sense? What if they get stumped on a question at home or in class? The following suggestions will help students settle the amygdala and will prepare them to deal with these challenges:

1. Take a deep breath and allow your elevator doors to open.
2. Drink some water.
3. Do some chair pull ups.
4. If possible, get up and move around.
5. Give yourself a positive pep talk. "I can figure this out."
6. Reread the question.
7. Highlight the key words.
8. Identify any words in the question you do not understand.
9. Look up unclear words.
10. Read the rest of the questions; the answer to one question can be found in another question.
11. Read the question again.
12. Read the question emphasizing different words each time. You may need to read the question seven-ten times before it becomes clear to you.
13. Realize no one expects you to be perfect.
14. Take a mind trip back to the class. Visualize the teacher reviewing the worksheet or demonstrating the concept.
15. Arrive at school early to ask the teacher for

assistance.

16. During a test, if unfamiliar words make it impossible for you to answer the question, ask the teacher to define them.

As homework facilitators, we want to guide our students in learning how to activate the RAS and settle the amygdala.

Chapter 14
Different Learning Styles-
Different Study Methods

It is not important to label a learner, but the following information can help students identify which strategies will be most effective for them. They may discover that they do best with a variety of strategies. The following are simply guidelines for self-discovery:

Kinesthetic Learner

This student learns best through touch or by physical involvement with a concept. The following strategies prove very effective for the kinesthetic learner:

1. Writing ideas and concepts on note cards or heavy-duty paper.
2. Building a model.
3. Acting out a concept.
4. Tracing items.
5. Writing on a pad of paper as opposed to a sheet of paper.
6. Dancing to a beat while reciting facts or retelling information.
7. Bouncing on an exercise ball while memorizing.
8. Throwing a ball at a target while memorizing.
9. Bouncing a ball while memorizing.
10. Using rice or other tactile material and your index finger to practice writing facts or spelling words.
11. Using a twister disc to practice memorization or to gather thoughts.
12. Filling in a diagram or creating a flow chart.
13. Using a soft lead pencil when studying material.
14. Writing on construction paper over sandpaper when studying words or facts.
15. Using lip movement during silent reading.
16. Reading while riding a stationary bike or walking on a treadmill.
17. Jumping rope to aid in memorization.

Visual Learner

This student learns best by using methods that offer strong visual clues. The following activities will enhance this learner's performance:

1. Writing and outlining study material.
2. Graphing.
3. Diagramming.
4. Using flashcards.
5. Configuration clues.
6. Highlighting key terms.
7. Utilizing visualization techniques for retrieval of information.
8. Color-coding concepts.
9. Using mind maps or graphic organizers.
10. Creating pictures of concepts.
11. Creating cartoons of concepts.
12. Webbing.
13. Using flow charts with various colors to distinguish steps and common concepts.
14. Observing what does not appear to be correct when studying new spelling words and highlighting what does not seem to fit.

Auditory Learner

This student learns best by hearing or talking about concepts. This student will benefit from the following study strategies:

1. Taping lectures and listening to them several times.
2. Reading material aloud.
3. Talking through tasks.
4. Orally summarizing what has been read.
5. Looking for similar sound patterns in new words.
6. Memorizing by reciting repetitively.
7. Discussing concepts with classmates or parents.
8. Reading questions aloud, emphasizing different words each time.
9. Turning material into patterns using mnemonic devices.
10. Creating a song incorporating all the material and singing it.
11. Writing a rhyme using key points.

Chapter 15
Personality Matters

Extrovert, Introvert or Ambivert?

Selecting an appropriate place to study depends on each student's personality. There are three basic personality styles: extrovert, introvert and ambivert. The best way to understand these styles is to think of a battery. Some of us are born with fully charged batteries. Others are born with little charge, while the batteries of others are about 50% charged.

Charging our batteries can occur in different fashions. We charge our batteries through contact with others, either through physical proximity or by talking to them. Even the TV can offer a charge. We can also charge our batteries by listening to music.

We discharge our batteries by spending time alone, exercising or by listening to soothing music.

The Extrovert

Students who are extroverts lack a charge or have little charge. They like going to school for the interaction with others. They will sit in the middle of the classroom and are perfectly happy being in the thick of things. The degree of charge they have will determine if they want more interaction when they get home, in which case they will still want to be with people.

Some extroverts can be with people all day and want to be with them in the evening as well. They tend to be the first people to arrive at a party and the last ones to leave. They develop very good social skills because they are always practicing. Interaction with others stimulates them; it is never tiring. In fact, they experience a euphoric feeling when around others.

Extroverts study best at home with others or in a library. They find studying in a crowded room or in front of the television more effective than in the solitude of their rooms. In fact, studying in the bedroom with no one around can feel isolating and painful. Extroverts want to know what is going on around them. The best place for these students to do homework might be in the living room or at the kitchen table, where they are in the center of activity. Being in the middle of the action is less distracting than being in their rooms. Noise does not always interfere with their concentration. In fact, many extroverts will tell you that they actually concentrate better with noise around them.

Because talking is a way to charge the extroverts' batteries, they often have trouble in class. Their desire to charge their batteries causes them to talk to their neighbor, often at the wrong time. Many extroverts spend many hours in detention due to talking in class. Offering strategies to stimulate themselves in other ways will improve the performance of these students. Chewing gum is an excellent tool to help stimulate their batteries. Squeezing a stress ball will offer the same type of stimulation.

Extroverts thrive on interaction with people. They study best with others. Study groups work well for them. Talking about the assignment on the phone with peers can also be an effective method. They like to talk. Allowing students to talk about what they have learned solidifies the concepts and accommodates their personality style. It reinforces the concept and allows them to socialize at the same time. If they are required to read books, they might find reading aloud to someone else a more effective way to get the task completed.

To encourage extroverts to establish good study habits, parents can study along with their children. This does not mean doing the child's work. It means doing the parent's "homework," which might be paying bills or personal reading—at the same time in the same room.

The Introvert

Introverts are born with a big charge. They do not experience the same challenges as extroverts, since they do not have a driving desire to talk to their neighbors. They find solace in the quiet of their rooms, where they can concentrate. They prefer sitting on the edge of the classroom. If they are put in the middle, they find it distracting. Often classrooms can be too noisy for them. During seatwork, using earplugs or a CD player with headphones can help them discharge.

When they arrive home, they are carrying a fully charged battery and often require discharging time. Quiet activity after school is best for these students. They are more inclined to say, "I need to be by myself." This allows them a cooling down period. Interacting can be exhausting for them.

Once they have settled their batteries, they will interact with others. They find studying alone in quiet locations most effective. A study group is rarely their choice for test preparation. They are often the first people to leave a party and become over energized by the interaction with others. Introverts are tired by the same activities that energize the extrovert.

The Ambivert

Ambiverts carry significant charges, yet do not require the charging time of extroverts nor the discharging time required by introverts. Ambiverts' study location choices will vary depending on their charge at the time. If their charge is full, they may want to be alone. If they are in need of charging, they might choose to study in the kitchen. A library is often their choice. It allows them to be with people, yet is quiet.

Allowing students to experiment with and evaluate choices will allow for the differences between their personalities and yours. Being aware that you are one personality type and your students can be different types is crucial to their success. What might work for you as a learner may be counter productive for your students' learning styles.

Sharing the battery theory with your students will help them identify their own styles. It is surprising how an understanding of this theory helps young students identify their learning styles. Students often comment, "I knew I needed to be in the kitchen to do my homework. I can't wait to tell my mom why."

Introverts who are children of extroverts are relieved to know nothing is wrong with them, because they don't enjoy studying with others. Extroverts are relieved to know why they like to talk at inappropriate times. Awareness is often all that is needed to curb their talking time. They will be sure to get their talking time during recess or at home.

Students' learning styles also affect how and when they study. Some students learn kinesthetically by interacting with concepts physically. They learn through dance or by writing concepts. Some students are auditory learners and absorb concepts by hearing them. Many students are visual learners and need to see concepts. Students employ a variety of modalities to learn best. Permitting experimentation allows them to determine the most effective strategies.

Students quickly identify which study methods and locations work best for them and which methods and locations are ineffective.

Chapter 16
Working Smarter, Not Harder

Students believe that studying means cramming all the information into their heads just before the test. If they perform well on the test they are operating under the misconception that they have mastered the information. Give them a pop quiz a month later and it will become clear how much information made it into their long-term memories. When presented with methods for study, they quickly see that cramming is working against them. It doesn't provide for long-term retrieval and it causes the amygdala to go crazy. Students need strategies for study. The following are some suggestions that have proven effective:

1. Before you begin to read material, determine how you will be tested on it. This will make a difference in how you read it and record information to study later on.
2. Form questions about the chapter and do browsing steps to ready your brain to receive information.
3. Read the chapter, highlighting key terms and concepts.
4. Make note cards.
5. When chapter two is assigned, take a few moments to look at the note cards for chapter one.
6. When chapter three is assigned, take a few minutes to look at the note cards for chapters one and two. This pattern continues for the ten weeks of the semester. (This process provides students with ten exposures to the information for chapter one, which keeps the pathways wide open. Since chapter ten is the most recently covered material, it will not require the same amount of review.)

When the material is not reviewed at all, students need to reread each of the previous chapters to be prepared for the final. Spending a few minutes weekly simply looking at note cards and placing the cards they know well in one pile and the ones that need review in another will save time in the long run.

Students will easily see the benefit of this review. It will keep the weeds from growing over their paths to retrieval. When asked which they would rather do, read the chapter and then a week before the final have to reread ten chapters, or make note cards and look at them five minutes a week, they prefer making the note cards.

After a one-week break from school, my math students were amazed at how quickly the paths to their long-term memories could become overgrown. They quickly determined that a little practice each night made sense. I did not need to remind them to practice. They knew what it would feel like if they did not practice. One student commented, "I am not going to let those weeds grow. I'm going to practice every night."

Effective Math Practice

Many teachers assume that children need many problems a night to attain mastery. Twenty math problems a night are not required to give students this type of practice. It is much more effective to assign five problems a night to be done accurately. When students are asked whether they would like to do twenty problems or five problems accurately, guess which option they choose? Our goal is for our students to attain mastery and ultimately to answer one problem on a standardized test, not twenty, and that answer needs to be accurate. Homework can provide the opportunity for them to practice this accuracy and learn how to self-check for accuracy.

Studying a Chapter

The following checklist will assist students in learning how to study a chapter of material:

1. If possible, preview the material before the class begins studying the chapter. This is the first step in studying. When the material is covered in class, it will serve as the second exposure.
2. Preview the Chapter:
    a. Look at the headings, captions and bold-faced words.
    b. Form questions about the material. What do you hope to learn from the chapter? Continue to ask yourself questions about what you are reading.
    c. Read the questions at the end of the chapter. (This focuses reading and improves comprehension. It helps students determine the main ideas of the text.)

d. Study any photos, graphs or charts and draw conclusions about them.

3. Read each paragraph, stopping to summarize or paraphrase. Sticky notes are a great way to record key words and main ideas. (To record information, students must focus on what is being read; this transforms them from passive readers to active readers.)
4. Organize your sticky notes using any of the following methods: outline, note cards, time line, charts, webs, venn diagrams or cartoon strips of information, or create a mnemonic device to assist in retention.
5. Answer all questions provided by the textbook and/or teacher.
6. When taking notes, use only one side of the paper.
7. Rewrite notes taken in class and turn them into note cards or an outline. Use different colors for different ideas. Use as few words as possible.
8. If you have difficulty placing a concept on an index card, ask the teacher to help you understand the material and break it down into smaller parts.
9. Continually check your understanding.
10. When the teacher returns your worksheet, determine what you did not understand. Be able to clearly describe the types of errors you made. If you are unclear about why a problem is marked wrong, discuss it with the teacher. Create a note card for the corrected information.

Preparing for a Test

Students are not born with study strategies. Offer them several alternatives for studying material and allow opportunities to fail so they can find the strategy that works for them. The following are just a few of the choices that can be offered:

1. Use note cards to study.
2. Study with a friend and reteach the concepts to each other.
3. Create possible essays based on the quizzes and worksheets.
4. Create fill-in quizzes and take them.
5. Turn your note cards into quiz cards. Number them

and number your paper to match. Write the answer to the note card. Then check your answers by turning the note card over.

6. Ask a parent or friend to quiz you on the material.
7. Review any charts or graphs you created. Form a mental picture of all parts.
8. Reread the chapter into a tape player and listen to it several times.
9. Form mental pictures of all concepts.
10. Review your material just before you go to bed and check your understanding upon awakening.
11. The quizzes tell you what you didn't know. Review the problems you missed and determine the correct answers.

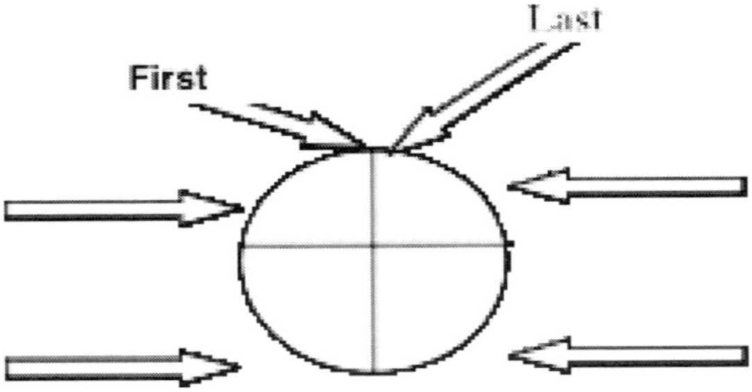

Studying for One Hour

Our strongest memories are of our first and last study experiences. If we study for one hour, we only have one first and last experience. If we break that study into four fifteen-minute segments, we will have eight first and last experiences. Encourage your students to break up their study sessions. (The schedule provided in the Appendix is broken into fifteen-minute segments).

Chapter 17

Effective Goal Setting

A

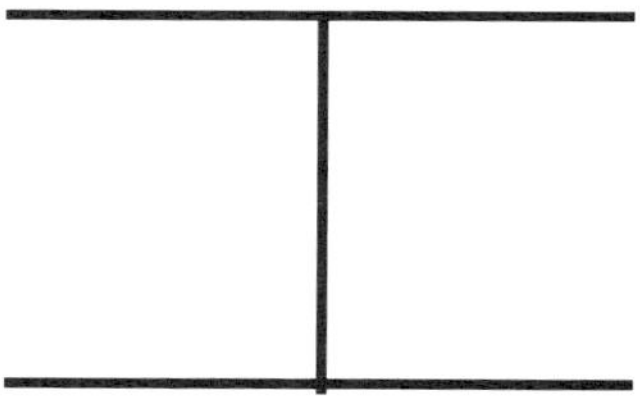

B

Goal setting will help students maximize their success. They will not see the value of a goal until goals are explained in terms they can understand. Using the diagram above, ask your students which field they would prefer to play on during recess. Most students will respond that field B would be their choice. When asked why, the most common answer is because it has goals. When asked why the goal is so important, students agree that without goals you do not know if you have won.

This can then be connected to school. If students don't know where they are going, they won't know when they have arrived. If they can visualize themselves accomplishing a goal, their subconscious minds will drive them in the direction of that goal.

Visualizing the grades they want to achieve by the end of the semester is not enough. They need to define what it will take to achieve the grades they want. Providing them with guidelines for earning grades will help them stay on track. Grading can be very subjective, which will make it hard for students to stay focused. Clearly defined objectives will offer a target to shoot for.

Identifying goal-blocking behaviors is essential for the success of this program. Students list three specific goals on a piece of paper. They must be observable goals. They cannot say, "I will work harder this year." The goal must be stated in observable behavior, such as "I will record my homework every night and turn it in on time." Then they are asked to list all the behaviors that would get in their way, based on previous experience. My list included:

1. I talk too much in class.
2. My desk is messy and that makes it hard to find my papers.

1. I will doodle instead of talking. I will not sit next to anyone I might talk with during class.
2. I will stop myself from shoving my papers in my desk. I will make sure that I place my papers in the folders for storing my work.

As students move through the year, they will continue to look at their goals weekly and create new goal-achieving behaviors as they encounter new challenges.

Morgan was an eighth grader who was not completing his homework and forgetting to get projects completed. He met with me to help him get organized. He made a list of his goal-blocking behaviors. The first item on his list was "I play too late and then I run out of time to do my homework." The second item was "I lose track of time when the teacher assigns a project and before I know it, it is due." He quickly recognized what was getting in his way. He came up with a strategy to solve the first challenge. He decided to do his homework as soon as he got home and then play basketball. He said that since it gets dark early, he would play for twenty minutes and then do homework. If there was time after he finished his homework, he would play again.

Being in control of the decision making about what he was going to do motivated him to make it work. He needed assistance in long-range planning, but now he was motivated because he was deciding on the schedule. This also removed his mother from nagging him. He admitted that he would stay outside at times just to get her mad. Once that element of control was removed, he experienced success. He felt he had power and he didn't want to lose it.

Self evaluations are another form of goal setting. After each major project, test or presentation, allot time for students to evaluate how they prepared, if they were happy with their performance and what changes they will make for future assignments of the same nature. Learning is an ongoing process. This exercise is very powerful in bringing about significant change in student performance.

Goal Setting Sheet

Proper Prior Planning Prevents Poor Performance

Name________________________________

Date________________________________

Goal for this
trimester____

____

____

____

____

1. List the behaviors that might get in the way of achieving your goal.

____

____

____

____

____

2. Restate #1 statements as positive behaviors.

____

____

____

____

____

____

____

____

____

____

____

____

After they have their goal-blocking behaviors listed (and they will be surprisingly accurate if given permission to be honest), they create a new list by changing them into goal-achieving behaviors. The following is my goal-achieving list:

Name____________________ Date________________

Activity____

Describe how you studied for this test or prepared for this presentation.

Describe changes you will make in preparation for the next test or presentation.

What did you learn from the errors you made on this test or presentation?

Chapter 18
The Power of Feelings

The power of identifying feelings is essential to the effectiveness of this program. Students will continually be asked to identify how an action made them feel. Being aware that they have control over whether they feel good or bad at any given time will make this system work effectively. Pain is a valuable tool, as long as students are redirected with strategies to avoid pain in the future. Once this change of behavior occurs and pain is replaced with pleasure, students will be more likely to avoid repeating mistakes.

As educators, we need to make the most of every failure. Identifying the feelings associated with the perceived failure and redirecting students will give us power as facilitators. Students often do not realize that they are in control of their feelings. Many students have become accustomed to placing blame on others when they have performed poorly or think others hurt their feelings. Consequently, they don't connect with the idea that they ultimately hold the power to changing how they feel. The positive side effect of this program is that students discover the power of their thoughts and how they can control the feelings they experience by the choices they make. It's POWERFUL!!!

♦

Should I let my child have a friend FAX forgotten homework?
Consider FAXing as an enabler. If they can rely on someone else, they will not learn a successful pattern. The pain of forgetting is much more powerful and will bring about lasting change. We don't want them relying on others forever.

Parents need some coaching. The following letter explains how they can support their children in the learning process. We want to train parents to see the progress their children are making and focus on the process and not the end product.

♦

Dear Parents:

Attached is a copy of your child's first Social Studies test. We reviewed the test and discussed appropriate answers. Each child was given the opportunity to improve his/her score by correcting all errors. I modeled the proper paragraphs and encouraged the students to make corrections by rewriting their answers. If they were satisfied with their performance, there was no need to make any changes. After they corrected their work, they evaluated their own performance.

The purpose of this activity is to bring into the children's awareness the need to learn from performance and prescribe a change for future tests. Each child decided what he/she did correctly and decided how he/she would improve performance on the next test. Please encourage your child to share what he/she learned.

The students performed well. The first experience with a Social Studies test can be stressful, but the children rose to the occasion and performed well. They applied different strategies to determine how they learn best.

I would like to keep this test as reference, so your child can review it before the next test. Please sign and return it in the parent folder.

Sincerely,

Ms. O

♦

When we remove parents from the process of homework, we need to increase our communication, reassuring them that their children are performing according to expectations.

♦

Chapter 19
Consequences

Students need to experience negative consequences when they do not complete their homework. Along with missing recess or doing detention, students need counseling. They need to be empowered with strategies for avoiding challenges over and over again. Students would be more successful if they knew how. They often do not know why they are having difficulties. Using the following form, provide time for students to evaluate mistakes and create an action plan for changing behavior.

Hall of Fame is a perfect time to use the initial goal-setting process of identifying goal-blocking behaviors and changing them into goal-achieving behaviors. This is an on-going process during the year. During the Hall of Fame session, students share their challenges and their plan for change. If challenges are worth sharing with the entire class, we discuss them on Monday, so every student can benefit from those who missed Hall of Fame.

Hall of Fame

I missed Hall of Fame today, _______________200___.

I missed Hall of Fame because:

Is this the first time you have made this mistake?

Describe how you feel about missing the assignment and missing Hall of Fame.

What behavior will you change to avoid making this mistake again? Describe the actions you will take to avoid making this mistake.

Spend the remainder of Hall of Fame visualizing the changed behavior.

Chapter 20
Dismantling Power Struggles

Power struggles occur when students feel they have no power. They will attempt to express it in negative ways if they are not given more control. Many students are in power struggles with their parents. Placing students in control of their planning, of day planners, of scheduling study time and managing their personal materials gives them the power and they will use it wisely. If they are making the decisions, they are more likely to make them work. After all, wouldn't you do anything you could to make your idea work? Students are no different. The idea can be far fetched, but does not matter. If it is their idea, they are going to make it work.

A third-grader named Erik is a perfect example of this theory. Erik had been unsuccessful at homework and his mother was frustrated. She had bought into our program, but Erik had not. He told his mother he had it under control and that she wasn't supposed to ask him about his homework. Clearly he wanted control, yet he wasn't using it to his advantage. He had missed every Hall of Fame for two months. Some of his peers had missed one or two; others hadn't missed any. He was the only one in the third grade who had decided to misuse his power. Each week he offered another challenge the class learned from, yet he lacked the motivation to be consistent and establish the skills he needed to be successful.

The next day, he did not turn in all his work because he had not recorded every assignment completely. Because he was in a power struggle with his mother, I had leverage. The following conversation changed his performance for the rest of the year:

"Erik, you have made many mistakes. Mistakes are a part of learning, but yours indicate that you need help at home. Your math teacher doesn't think you can do your work on your own and wants to call your mother and have her monitor you at home. Do you want that? I don't think you need your mother's help, but she does. Is she right or am I?"

"You are."

"The only way we will know that I am correct is if you begin recording your homework yourself and turning in completed work. Can you do that yourself?"

"Yes!"

"How do you plan to be successful?"

"I am going to record my homework and make sure I have

everything I need before I leave class. I'm also going to look at my homework carefully to be sure I know how to do everything before I leave the class. Then I am going to do my work as soon as I get home."

"I will give you a chance to prove that Mrs. S is wrong. If you don't change your behavior, we will have to pull your mother into the picture. I will be checking you daily. I know you can do this."

Erik did not miss a homework assignment for the rest of the year. In fact, his mother remarked that his behavior improved at home and that he was sharing more with her. He even asked her to listen to him practice his presentation. Another benefit of placing him in control reduced the tension at home and improved interpersonal relations with his parents.

Will had not had success with homework for three months. His teacher and mother had come up with several suggestions to help him. They were excellent suggestions, but unfortunately none of them worked. I was called in to work with Will.

In a parent/student/teacher session, it became clear that Will was in a power struggle with his teacher and mother. He was asked to define what was getting in his way. Of course, he replied with the standard, "I don't know." We convinced him that we were prepared to spend as many recesses as necessary together for him to figure it out. Until this point, every time he said, "I don't know," his teacher or parent would identify the challenge for him. He could get off the hook and go out and play. But I was not going to give him any solutions. He needed to be more actively involved in the process.

It is important for students to identify problems for themselves, which they will if given time. He thought about his friends on the playground and quickly announced, "I guess I don't start on it when I get home and then I don't feel like doing it." He was asked to prescribe what he could do to solve his challenge. He again responded with, "I don't know." This response always bought him more time. The teacher and parent would prescribe a change and he could go out and play. This time he wasn't going to get off that easily. I informed him that I had plenty of time to sit with him until he could figure this one out. "How are you going to get yourself to do your homework?" I asked.

"I guess I just need a sign above my desk that says, "Do it now."

"Do you think that will work?"

"Yep, and I'll make the sign on my computer."

From that day on, Will never forgot his homework. It was his decision and no one else's. In the past, he didn't care if his teacher's or mother's ideas were successful. But now, he couldn't let his idea fail.

Many years later, I saw him in the hall. He was about to graduate from middle school. I asked him how the homework was going, and his reply was, "The sign still works." After graduating from high school, he came back for a visit and informed me that he was taking the sign to put up in his college dorm.

I don't think Will ever realized it wasn't the sign that made the difference; it was his decision that made the difference.

◆

When students feel no power, they will gain it any way they can. If it means not doing an assignment to exercise that power, they will.

◆

"School is like riding a bike. If you never take off the training wheels, you never learn that you can ride the bike with just two wheels. If children always have help, they will never learn what they can do on their own."

Victoria Olivadoti

Chapter 21
Dealing with Frustration

Students deal with frustration in various ways. Some will cry and some will avoid the work. Neither solution is appropriate or effective, yet they are the only ways students know to respond to the stressors that create frustration. Staging situations and demonstrating how to deal with them will teach students to deal with feelings of frustration. It is much more effective to talk about how frustration feels and how to deal with it when students are calm. They will be less receptive when they are upset.

It is also important to realize that this is a learned behavior. Students have received feedback from past experience that it is okay to respond to stressors in this manner. Students are often surprised that there is another, more effective, way to deal with the feelings that cause frustration. We need to instruct students in effective stress-relieving strategies.

When faced with the need to answer a question they do not know, some students freeze up. In many cases, students who feel they must do well or they will get into trouble or not get an "A" put such pressure on themselves that they forget everything. These students often do not realize that they can skip a problem and return to it later. Sharing with students how stress affects performance, as described in Chapter 13, will help them understand why their brains go blank and is enough to get them to relax when they encounter a question they can't answer.

My father-in-law often tries to remember the name of someone about whom he wants to tell a story. He is known to say, "I can't remember the man's name. I should know it!" This creates a chemical change in the brain, blocking the information. When he relaxes enough to continue his story and doesn't focus on finding the name, it clearly pops into his head. He changed his thinking and sent his brain searching for the answer and it found it. The more you try to remember something in a stressful situation, the less likely it is that you will find the information.

Students can identify with the following story that I refer to many times during the year. “Have you ever tried opening an elevator door once it has begun to close? You have to pry it open or wait for the next elevator.” Our brains are like elevator doors. The way we close the pathway from our long-term memory file cabinet to the working memory desktop is by allowing ourselves to freak out if we come across something we think we should know but have forgotten. If you feel your elevator doors starting to close, simply take a deep breath and give the elevator a chance to go to the next floor. Waiting to relax will help the elevator doors to your brain open. Going on to the next problem and reassuring yourself that you know this information will help to open your doors. The key to keeping your doors open is to relax and not let challenges frustrate you. Putting too much pressure on yourself to do things perfectly is a sure way to close those doors.

There are many ways to deal with a question or problem you do not know how to answer. One may be in the form of another question, or skip the problem and the answer will come to you. Take a deep breath and say to yourself, “I know this stuff and the answer will come to me.” Thinking you do not have the answer occupies your brain and prevents you from retrieving the information. Giving the brain the positive message that you can find the answer will help the answer come to you.

We need to be sure that we are not creating frustration for students. My niece recalls when she asked what she considered to be a thoughtful question and her teacher’s response was, “You are smart; go figure it out.” It is more effective to train students to reread the question, so they can “figure it out.” It takes a great deal of courage for students to admit that they do not understand a concept or question. We need to respect that courage and realize they may not have the techniques to figure it out, no matter how bright they are. Chances are that there are several other students (who are not confident enough to ask) not understanding. For each student who asks how to do a problem, we must assume there are others who fear asking.

We also need to examine how we feel about comments such as “I don’t get it.” Our response to students usually has tension behind it. After all, we did a great job of teaching the concept and any fool should understand. I used to feel my blood boil when a student responded this way.

Once my thinking and my response changed, I observed a change in students’ responses. When they said, “I don’t get it,” instead of berating them and responding “Why weren’t you listening?” I changed my reaction to “What part of the concept do you not understand? Could you be more specific?”

Students need to be taught how to get it on their own. When

asked which part of the question they did not understand, the "and" or the "the," they laugh and look at the problem differently. Once they are taught to focus on what they did not understand, fewer students say "I don't get it."

Stories of successful people struggling will also help students to relax, be more comfortable with not being perfect and experience less stress. Sharing the Edison story is very helpful. Like Thomas Edison, if something is not working well, instead of getting frustrated, students need to try again and again until they get it. Edison worked on the filament for the light bulb for many years. He tried 1,000 ways until he found the one that worked. He didn't feel he had failed 999 times. They were just ways that did not work and he was looking for the one way that did. Aren't you glad he didn't give up after 999 tries? If he had, we would be studying by candlelight.

Another story that is great to share centers on basketball. Connecting with students requires us to know their affinities. If my class enjoys basketball, I share the story of Michael Jordan. Michael Jordan was a determined boy. His high school coach told him that he was not good enough for the team. He could have given up, but he desperately wanted to be on the team. He decided to practice and show the coach that he belonged on the team. He made a choice and decided to set a goal. He later proved he was worthy of being on the team and the rest is history. How do you think he accomplished his goal? By practicing. He proved that proper prior practice prevents poor performance. He didn't give up when it got hard; he kept at it.

I once had a student who responded that Michael Jordan learned to become a good basketball player by watching others play. In some respects he was correct. Michael had to know what made a good player. Our students need to know what a good student looks like. They need it clearly defined. They also need to be taught how it feels to practice stress-relieving strategies. They need to know it and practice it before they need it. They also need to be aware that stress happens to everyone. It's how we deal with it that makes the difference.

Many times students do not know how to cope with frustration. Parents often feed into the frustration by validating it. When we read the problem or explain the directions, we are sending the message that frustration is a bad thing and that the only way to deal with it is to get help. To foster a problem-solving attitude, we need to send the message that frustration is a very important part of problem solving. How we deal with frustration will determine how successful we become in solving our problems.

At the first sign of frustration, provide strategies that will empower rather than enable. It is also important to remember that when frustration sets in, students' creative abilities to problem solve are hindered. Telling the student "You know this stuff; figure it out" simply adds to the frustration. Identify that the lack of understanding can sometimes be a source of frustration. This will relieve the student's stress. Students are very receptive to problem-solving techniques if they are presented with compassion.

Frustration can also be created when we expect immediate responses to questions without allowing for adequate "thinking time." If neural paths are weak, retrieval will take longer. If students are not given adequate time to discover that they can retrieve the information, they develop a negative atttitude and experience frustration. They shut down and never learn that they could have retrieved the information if enough time had been alotted. Giving students time to record their answers on paper, until everyone has had time to record something, will reduce frustration. It will also alert the quick responders that there are often more than one answer or solution to a problem, and that given time, their answers and solutions can become more creative.

When we call on a child and expect an immediate response when they are not prepared to be called upon, the stress response kicks in and they can't remember the information, even if they knew it well. Having students record their ideas on paper first, allows them to have options if called upon. For this reason is it suggested to only call on students who raise their hands.

Students' frustration levels will increase when they are told that their homework shouldn't take them the amount of time it is taking. One student shared with her teacher that her homework was taking her three hours each everning. Her teacher's response was, "It shouldn't be taking you that long." There were no solutions offered to deal with the time, and the teacher did not offer to examine why the homework was taking so much time. Whether it should or shouldn't didn't matter. What matters is that it did! The stress caused by this situation intensified the student's frustration, negatively impacting her ability to focus in class and resulted in her homework taking her even longer.

I am a strong believer in demystification. Being frank with students about their disabilities and the power they possess to deal with them is key to their success. It is important to let students in on what happens when a method of dealing with a problem is ineffective. Students already know what is difficult for them; they don't always know why or how to change it. Sharing the why without making excuses will empower students. Offering strategies to deal with their challenges reduces stress. They often don't realize that their reactions to difficulty can change the result, and with simple strategies, what was once hard can now become easy.

Beware of Confabulation

Confabulation is the brain's way of taking bits of information and making sense of them. Children confabulate in classrooms daily. Give them plenty of opportunity to check their thinking. They sometimes compile disconnected bits of information and connect them inaccurately. They are not wrong; they are confabulating. Alert students to the dangers of confabulation.

Proper Prior
Planning
Prevents
Poor Performance

Proper Prior Practice
Prevents Poor
Performance

Chapter 22

Teaching Scheduling

Time management is a skill that is often neglected because there are so many other demands on teachers' time. Projects are assigned and dates are given to students, yet they are never taught how to manage the dates. The dates are not internalized and result in students waiting until the last minute to complete assignments. If they knew how to do it differently, they would. Students need assistance in managing hours, days and weeks before we can expect them to manage months and quarters.

The first stage of this program requires a day-to-day strategy. This allows students to establish a nightly pattern for homework. Once they establish an internal time management system for each day, they are ready for two-day projects. Eventually they can manage monthly projects. Programs that begin with weekly packets do not encourage a nightly homework plan and inadvertently encourage procrastination. If the work is due on Friday, the student lacking natural organizational skills will not do the work until Thursday night. Many students have paper management issues, so giving them a packet that requires adult management does not develop the independence that is gained by a structured program.

The nightly program is recommended until students are successful. It allows them to deal with challenges before they become bigger issues. When they are able to manage one nightly assignment, gradually add to the nightly assignments until students are doing three assignments an evening.

Then we begin assignments that are due in two days. Gradually we move to three-day assignments and eventually, we assign work on Monday that is due Friday, while students continue to complete nightly assignments. Once students have mastered the weekly assignment, we are ready to teach the scheduling of a monthly book report.

Step 1: Minute Minding

The first issue to be addressed is timing and scheduling. When students ***learn how to plan***, it helps them ***plan to learn***. They need to know if their understanding of time is askew. Begin by having them close their eyes and raise their hands when they think two minutes have elapsed. You will find that many do not have a realistic understanding of a minute and therefore have an even less accurate understanding of fifteen minutes or a half-hour. The time between December 1 and December 25 seems like an eternity. Therefore, it stands to reason they will feel that they have a lot of time when assigned a project a month in advance.

To get students "real on time" requires them to record the beginning and ending time for each of their assignments. My motive is to get them "real" about the actual time it takes to complete their homework. I love it when students say, "My homework took me an hour last night." When they record the beginning and ending times the next evening they discover that it may have seemed like an hour, but in reality it was only twenty minutes.

Asking for time feedback also gives the teacher valuable information about the actual time the activity takes and helps to determine if the appropriate amount of homework is being assigned. The following is the dialogue used to prepared them for this task: "I would like your assistance this evening in determining if I am giving the correct amount of homework. I need you to do your homework in a specific fashion for me to be sure. Please record the time you begin your assignment, stay focused while you are doing it and record the time you complete the assignment. Do this for each assignment. I will use the information I collect from the class to determine if I am assigning the appropriate quantity of work. Can I count on your help?" If we discover that the homework is taking too much time, we need to adjust the amount assigned. Students are eager to help you. In return, you are teaching them the concept of time and making allowance for their needs.

Setting the stage for the acceptance of individual differences contributes to the success of this program. Before the students share the amount of time it took for them to complete their assignments, preface the session by stating, "You will find that some of you completed the assignment in five minutes, while others took twenty minutes to complete the same assignment. This is not a race and time differences are expected. Everyone works at his own pace. Often students work too quickly and make needless mistakes, while those who take a little longer find they make fewer mistakes. We are looking for the time that it takes to do this assignment accurately. If you find that the assignment took you a lot longer than your classmates, we can discuss some strategies to help speed you up a little later." If we offer solutions, we can help students manage their time more effectively. If we assign too much homework we are less likely to have attentive children in class, and what we hope to accomplished will not be possible. Children need time to play and socialize. If they don't they will take in during class time.

Step Two: Deciding on a Time and Place to Study

The next step is to empower students by assisting them in scheduling their daily assignments. Your students need to decide on a time that is best for them to do their homework. Some students need a break right after school and some need to do their homework right away.

Students need the opportunity to decide where and when they will study and then evaluate the effectiveness of their choices. To assist them in making informed decisions, they list their activities for the week on a weekly time chart that allows space for recording all extracurricular activities. We begin with the first day and use a daily calendar broken into fifteen-minute increments. A template is provided on pages 100 and 101.

A

3:00-3:15	
3:15-3:30	
3:00-3:45	
3:45-4:00	
4:00-4:15	
4:15-4:30	
4:30-4:45	
4:45-5:00	
5:00-5:15	
5:15-5:30	
5:30-5:45	
5:45-6:00	
6:00-615	
6:15-6:30	

B

3:00-3:15	Drive Home
3:15-3:30	
3:30-3:45	Snack
3:45-4:00	
4:00-4:15	Soccer Practice
4:15-4:30	Soccer Practice
4:30-4:45	Soccer Practice
4:45-5:00	Soccer Practice
5:00-5:15	
5:15-5:30	
5:30-5:45	
5:45-6:00	
6:00-6:15	
6:15-6:30	

C

3:00-3:15	Drive Home
3:15-3:30	Snack
3:30-3:45	Find Shoes, Dress
3:45-4:00	Drive to Practice
4:00-4:15	Soccer Practice
4:15-4:30	Soccer Practice
4:30-4:45	Soccer Practice
4:45-5:00	Soccer Practice
5:00-5:15	Drive Home
5:15-5:30	Eat Dinner
5:30-5:45	
5:45-6:00	
6:00-6:15	Pick up Dog's Mess
6:15-6:30	

When filling in the schedule, students need to consider the

amount of time necessary to prepare for activities, including dressing time and travel time to and from home. They also need to schedule chores, dinner, bath time and anything else they plan to complete each afternoon and evening. When students look at the "Sample A" time sheet, it looks like they have a lot of time to complete the assignments. Even after they fill in the activities and write in when they are going to complete each assignment, to students who suffer from time management dysfunction, the white space looks like free time. They often do not consider everything required to get ready and travel time involved. When students begin filling in these schedules, they will look like "Sample B." By adding dressing time and travel time and by highlighting the times that are **unavailable** for homework, as in "Sample C," and not highlighting spaces that are available to complete homework and other activities, students can clearly see how much available time they have. Highlighting the unavailable time gives students a precise visual. It is very powerful and is it is not unusual for students to see how little time they have and they become motivated to get started on their work during their recess or lunch times. They see time in a way that makes total sense to them. Try highlighting the unavailable time in "Sample C" with a yellow highlighter right in this book and see what happens. It's amazing, isn't it?

Students who suffer from time management dysfunction do not consider possible issues that will eat up time. They know that they go to practice from five to six, but they fail to plan for the preparation time. If they have problems managing papers, there is a good chance they don't manage their clothes any better. Alert them to the fact that they need to plan for the time it takes to find their clothing, get dressed, drive to practice, practice and drive home. This can take up to forty-five minutes more than they had planned.

Completing afternoon hourly schedules for the first two weeks creates time awareness. They realize very quickly that prior proper planning prevents poor performance. They begin making choices that help them be successful. For example, if students have cotillion or soccer practice after school, they may decide to get started on their homework during recess or in the car during carpool. Students who plan well do not find themselves in a bind and are able to follow a process that will guarantee the success of this program.

After we discuss the homework completely, they are to fill a daily schedule for five days. Through the use of the daily schedule they can predict what the rest of the week will look like and determine if they need to work ahead. The following dialogue is used to introduce this process:

"You are going to decide right now when and where you think you should do your homework. First, you need to record all your planned activities. If you have soccer practice, highlight the time you will be at practice. Since you have to travel to and from practice, highlight that time also. Highlight the time you need to get ready for practice. Now record the time you set aside for chores, piano or other instrument practice, dinner, bath or whatever you do daily. Be sure to highlight the time slots. Now you know the times available for homework.

"Some students need time to play outside as a break from schoolwork, so they do their homework after playing for a while. Others might want to get the work done and then play, so they don't have the homework gnawing at them. I do not recommend postponing the homework to the next morning. Why do you suppose?"

Students eventually realize that leaving homework to the next morning may not give them enough time to get ready for school and finish the assignment. Mornings are stressful enough; they don't need to add homework to other morning activities.

"Using your schedule for this afternoon, decide on the times that are available to do your homework and plan for it now. If you have only from 3:45 p.m. to 4:45 p.m. available, you might not be able to schedule any play time. If you have three or four blank spaces on your schedule, you can decide when you will plan your play time and when you will plan your homework. Remember to record ten minutes of fact practice and twenty minutes of silent or partner reading.

"You must also decide where you are going to study. If you like being around people and your parents allow you to sit at the kitchen table, you might decide to do your homework there. If you need quiet, you might decide to do the homework at your desk. Some students like sitting at a desk, while others enjoy sitting on the floor or their beds.

"Many students do best with Baroque music playing in the background, while some prefer the family talking around them. Still others require complete silence. They might even choose to use earplugs to help them concentrate. Whatever setting you choose, it must allow you to complete your homework in no more than one hour. If it takes longer, you will have to reconsider your choices. You will have to test out different locations to see which works best for you. Record where you are going to study at the top of this paper.

"When deciding when you are going to do an assignment, consider the way the brain works. If you do not like a subject, you are sending a message to your brain not to do it. Knowing this, which do you think would be the best one to do first? You are right. It is best to do the thing you like the least as your first assignment. Look at your schedule. Since studying words for spelling or vocabulary is best done just before you go to sleep, when should you schedule your vocabulary?" (Take student responses.)

"That's right, just before bedtime. Then you will have a better chance of storing the words in your long-term memory. If you have only fifteen minutes, what is an activity you can do in that amount of time?" (Take student responses.) "Practicing a fact of the day or focusing on a difficult word would be a good use of that time."

Every child needs down time. Scheduling it is very important. If they use their time wisely, they should be rewarded with time to do nothing at all or play a game. Instead of limiting their playtime, allow them to schedule it in and then evaluate the effectiveness of their choice. Many children learn quickly that playing first often makes it difficult to complete assignments. When they feel the stress of not being able to complete work because they played too late, they will recognize the need for other alternatives. I do not encourage the use of video or computer games because of its effect on the brain chemistry of a child. Because it changes the brain chemistry and makes it more difficult to concentrate, I encourage children to schedule their video games at a time when they will not need to concentrate afterwards. Because it robs the brain of dopemine, the chemical in your brain that aids in concentration, it makes one "brain dead" afterwards. Using such games after work makes more sense. Teens need time to talk to their friends. This should be scheduled.

This method of time management becomes internalized quickly. For even the most disorganized students, a week of using this schedule is adequate. Because it is so visual and because it makes sense, they begin getting real on time very quickly.

Sleep

Sleep is a crucial part of all aspects of learning. Most children today are not getting adequate sleep to help them store what they have learned during the day. Sleep deprivation can impact children for several days. The inability to attend is often linked to sleep deprivaton. When students recognize the storing of information is done during sleep, and without adequate sleep they will require more exposures to concepts, they will decide for themselves to go to bed at a reasonable hour. They will also plan to do a quieting activity before they go to bed to assist them in getting into a restful sleep.

A wonderful website on sleep is available to help students, parents and teachers understand the importance of sleep and the knowledge will motivate children to plan for adequate sleep. It is www.sleepforkids.org

Daily Schedules are
the Foundation for
Proper Prior Planning to
Prevent Poor Performance

3:00-3:15

3:15-3:30

3:30-3:45

3:45-4:00

4:00-4:15

4:15-4:30

4:30-4:45

4:45-5:00

5:00-5:15

5:15-5:30

5:30-5:45

5:45-6:00

6:00-6:15

6:15-6:30

6:30-6:45

6:45-7:00

7:00-7:15

7:15-7:30

7:30-7:45

7:45-8:00

8:00-8:15

8:15-8:30

8:30-8:45

Be sure to include brushing your teeth, bathing, eating dinner, walking the dog, skateboarding, playing Nintendo or taking out the trash. Remember to include time for friends and phone calls.

Arm your students with the language of success and the strategies to get their personal needs met from any teacher they may encounter.

Students of this program change every classroom they enter and every teacher they meet.

Chapter 23

The Art of Backward Planning

A Month Seems Like Forever Until You "Backward Plan"

Assigning projects can be overwhelming for students. Though it was mentioned earlier, it is worth repeating. **Many students think a month is a long time.**

Simply placing the due date in an agenda is not adequate for students who struggle with time management. Expecting parents to teach the planning is setting students up for failure. Many parents lack the skills we expect them to provide. If we want students to internalize the due dates, we must involve them in establishing due dates that work.

When asked how many days students need to practice for an oral presentation, the answers will vary from one to seven days. How can we present students with due dates without considering these scheduling differences and without teaching them the art of scheduling these differences for themselves?

The Book Report Process
A Long-Term Project

The book report can be a hellish experience for both students and parents. Students inevitably wait until the last minute to read the book, preventing them from completing the project in a timely fashion. Many teachers assign book reports but are unaware of how little time students have. It is unrealistic to expect students to read a 200-page book every month, do a project and complete their other assignments.

I use the plan described below to prevent poor planning and to determine whether students need more time to do a quality job. To do project planning we work backward. Students use their monthly calendar page to assign the due dates for various aspects of the book report. They rarely consider the time necessary to read the book.

The following items need to be considered when calendaring a book report:

1. All outside activities in detail, including weekend trips.
2. The steps involved in doing the project. If the project includes a poster, it will require a trip to the store for the materials and the time to design it. It will

also require the assistance of someone to take the student to the store, which should not be on the night before the project is due. If it is a written report, it will require a rough draft to be read and edited and then writing a final draft. This will require time for the teacher to read the rough draft and return it to the student. If it is a presentation, it will require practice time.

3. The book must be read.
4. The book must be chosen, which may require a trip to the bookstore or library. This too will require some assistance.

The following is an example of how to plan a book report schedule with your class:

"Today we are going to plan for a book report that will be due a month from today, March 30. You may think you have plenty of time to complete the report, but to keep you on track, we are going to create a calendar of projected due dates so you aren't completing the assignment on the night before it is due. I need each of you to calendar your activities for the next month. The dates on the board are no-school days because of intersession and holidays. Please calendar those dates along with your soccer games, campouts or family trips. Be sure to include any activity that will reduce your available evening or weekend time.

Your next job is to create a list of everything you must do to complete a book report of a non-fiction book of your choice. Now I would like you to work in teams of two or three and come up with all the steps you think are required to complete this project."

Give the teams adequate time to complete the list and then come together as a group. This activity requires every student to be actively involved. They all get a chance to think about the planning and when they get together they see the steps they may have missed.

The first time you do this activity it will be obvious which students would have been procrastinators and which would have completed the work early. If students cannot see all the steps naturally, the chances of failure are greater. As they listen to their peers, they are also checking their own thinking. This activity encourages active listening. If students are given a list, the procrastinators would not focus on it. When they have to create the list themselves, it has new meaning.

Scheduling has much greater impact when the students plan from the completed project backward. Instruct all students to visualize what their completed project will look like. Once they see the end product, they will be able to be successful.

"What is the **very last** thing your group came up with to complete this project? Let's make a list on the board."

"Turn in the project."

"When will you do that?"

"The day it is due."

"Can you turn in the project early?"

"Most students don't realize that they may turn in the project a few days early. If you do that and ask to have it reviewed to see if you are on the right track, what will the teacher most likely do?"

"Correct?"

"Teachers tend to correct what is given to them. You will have a better chance of getting a good grade by turning in the paper a few days before it is due so the teacher can look at it and tell you if you are missing anything. You need to allow enough time to make any changes before the actual due date. If your future teachers are anything like me, they won't be able to make the corrections right away. We are busy people and need at least three days. Therefore, what due date should you enter in your calendar?

The dates they offer vary since some need more time to make changes. Some of the students will choose March 25 as the due date. One student commented, "I'm going to put down March 20 because we have to count the weekends." As students become more involved in this process, their discussions help their peers see obstacles they might not have considered. Our discussion continues as follows:

"What is the next step?"

"To do the final draft."

"Record the number of days you will need for the final writing. What do you need to do before you can prepare the final draft?"

"Write the rough draft."

"Record the number of days you think you will need to do that. Just before the final draft you will need to do something else. What is it?"

"Have the rough draft proofread."

"Allow the teacher three days to do this. Before you write the rough draft and get it approved, what do you need to do? Do you understand the requirements of the project?"

"We'll have to learn how to do a book report."

"What is the next step?"

"Read the book."

"What do you need to do before you can do that?"

"Get the book."

"How many days do you think you will need to get the book? Do you need someone to take you to the library or a bookstore?

"I bet you thought doing a book report was easy. Now you have the following list of tasks before you can complete the assignment:

Turn in the project.
Do the final project.
Have the rough draft proofed.
Write the rough draft.
Read the book.
Get the materials for the project.
Get the book.

"Now we need to attach some dates to this project. Today is March 1 and your book review is due on March 30. How many days are available to complete this project?"

"30."

"Although each of your calendars is unique because you have different after school and weekend activities, the due date remains the same. Your due date for each step will not be same as your classmates' because each of you needs a different number of days to complete each part of the project. Since we discussed how valuable it is for the teacher to look at the final project a few days ahead of its due date, when should you record the due date for the final project?"

"March 25."

"Look at the number of days it will take you to rewrite the final copy. Back up that many days on the calendar and record, 'Do rewrite.' Look at the number of days you allowed for the teacher to proof your rough draft. Back up that many days and record, 'Ask teacher to edit.' You decided how many days you need to write your rough draft. Back up that many days on your calendar and record, 'Write rough draft.' Now look at your calendar.

"How many days do you have left to read the book? There appear to be fifteen to eighteen days left to read your book, based on all of your personal schedules. With this information, let's figure out how many pages you need to read each day to be successful. The fifteen days include weekend reading. If you don't want to read on the weekend, subtract four days. If there is a day of the week on which you don't have free time, subtract that many days. Now you know how many days you have to read your book. If it is fifteen days and you choose a book that is 150 pages long, you need to read ten pages a night. Is that workable? If you miss one night of reading, you will need to read eleven pages for ten of the nights and ten pages for five of the nights. Is this doable for you? If not, you will need to choose a different book. Every day you miss adds more pages to the other nights."

There are many aspects of project planning that the students don't consider. One is acquiring materials. If they have to rely on someone to take them to the library or store to pick up supplies and books, they need to be taught to think about it.

Alerting them to the need to plan for this will prevent last minute panic. Suggest they let a parent know right away that they will be doing a project in the next week and will need to go to the store to get supplies. Instructing them on how to ask for this support is helpful. They can ask their parents, "I am doing a project and need some supplies and a book from the library. When would be a good time for you to take me to the store and the library?" This is teaching them to plan ahead and also to show respect for their parents' time. When parents allow their children to convince them to run to the store at the last minute, they are sabotaging time management, so it is our job to teach the children how to manage their parents.

This activity, though time consuming, prevents procrastination, opens discussion and makes the activity and the dates meaningful for students. It helps them understand time and the need for thinking a project through. It is a powerful tool for teaching "Proper Prior Planning to Prevent Poor Performance" and prevents "The Night Before the Project's Due Nightmares."

After we have completed one such planning session together, the students do the next book report planning alone or in small groups and turn it in for review. By the third book report, they are scheduling independently. Even the most disorganized students can grasp this concept. It's inevitable that students will make scheduling errors the first time they plan alone, but that presents learning opportunities.

For the students with reading comprehension issues, suggest they use a sticky note after a page of reading and record a few words to remind them of what they read. This strategy improves reading comprehension by 75%. It reduces the time students waste by daydreaming. Summarizing after every page makes them accountable.

This project is not completed until the students evaluate their own progress. It is important to discuss how the scheduling went and if the students need to rethink the timing for their next project. After the project is completed ask the students to describe the challenges they faced and prescribe changes to avoid them in the future.

Sample of Project Planning

By teaching project planning we avoid unnecessary parent involvement and student procrastination. The project must have value. If it has educational value then it should first be modeled in the class so students can later apply the skill independently at home. Many teachers assign a project and then become angry when students fail to turn it in on time or turn in incomplete work. The teacher assumes the parents were not doing their job. After all, it's the parents' job to see that their students do the project.

There is a huge hole in this theory. First, parents may be no better equipped to organize the project than students. Parents may appear to be successful, yet if the project simply looks like busy work to them. If they lack the organizational skills to complete it, they dismiss the project by saying, "I didn't do well on this type of activity and I was still able to be successful."

When students are given specific instructions in processes that do not assume any prior knowledge, parents often learn skills they never acquired. Many parents have indicated that they learned more alongside their students in one year than during their own educations. By observing their own students, and not participating in the work, they have learned a process.

The planning for a project must begin with the entire class calendaring all the required activities. This is an interesting concept and seems to take more time than some teachers are willing to give, but the benefits are far reaching. Students are not handed a page of due dates. They will pay little attention to list of activities and their due dates. They are given a list of activities that are required to complete the project. They are asked to look at the list of activities and determine in what order they should be completed. The following project on an endangered animal is an example. After selecting an animal, the students are required to have the following work in their folders:

1. A postcard from the animal to another animal describing its habitat.
2. A business letter to someone who is causing the animal to become endangered, pleading for the animal's life and explaining the benefits of changing the situation so the animal can live.
3. A drawing of the animal in its habitat.
4. A diamante poem about the animal's diet.
5. A cinquain poem about what the student learned about the animal.
6. Notes taken from at least five sources about the animal.
7. A neatly written report from the student's notes.
8. A two- to five-minute oral report about the animal. The report must share something from each of the main topics of the student's report. The student can dress as the animal or as a scientist or journalist reporting on the animal.

"Today is February 5. The due date for this project is June 5. It may seem like you have a long time to do all this work, but as we schedule the activities you will see that you will need every single day and won't have time to waste. I would like you to decide which activities you should do first."

The following is an example of how the planning goes:

"Since June 5 is the due date, we need to enter that into our calendar first. We are going to plan backward to be sure we get everything completed before Open House.

Let's look at the last item, the Chit Chat about your animal. Is there anything you do not understand about the Chit Chat?" (The students ask questions to clarify exactly what is required, because by this time of the year they have done enough projects to know that if they don't have all the answers, they can't plan effectively.)

"Let's list everything you will need to do to prepare a talk on your animal."

You will review the required tasks and list them in reverse order.

1. Do the presentation.
2. Practice the presentation.
3. Write the presentation.
4. Have the teacher proofread the presentation.
5. Research and write notes about the animal.
6. Since you want dress as the animal, get a costume made.
7. Plan to get material and have your parent take you to the store to get poster paper for your information poster.

"Since everyone will be presenting their animal reports on June 5, on what date should you start practicing for this presentation? Do you need five days or twenty-five days of practice?" (Because the students began their Chit Chats in September, they will have had many opportunities to learn about the number of days they need to prepare for an oral presentation.)

"Consider how long your Chit Chats are going to be this time. They will be a lot longer than your previous ones."

The students decided to allow ten days for daily practice. They also need to consider whether to use a friend in the presentation because they learned from previous experience that they needed more practice time. The date they chose to begin practicing is May 26. They realized they could not depend on me to return their rough drafts the next day, so they chose to have the rough drafts due on May 21. They calendared a date to discuss the making of their costumes with whoever would be making it. They decided to do that right away, in case they wanted to learn to sew. They decided February 28 would be a good date to turn in their plans for costuming. The students became so adept at project challenges that they thought of things that hadn't crossed my mind.

To allow sufficient time for the teacher to correct and approve the Chit Chats, they assigned May 15 as the date to begin writing their reports. They knew that all the other parts of the project needed to be completed before they could even start on the oral report, so they began to see the time slipping away. I suggested they rate the remaining activities and do the easiest one last. They calendared the following due dates:

Final copy of postcard	May 13
Rough draft of postcard	May 11
Instructions for postcard	May 10
Right brain drawing	May 8
Final copy of letter	May 5
Rough draft of letter	May 1
Letter writing instruction	May 1
Final copy of poem	April 30
Rough draft	April 26 and 28
Instruction for poem	April 25 and 27
Computer cover	April 23
Illustrations with captions	April 22
Final copy of report	April 20
Rough draft of report	April 15
Note taking	April 10
Spring Break	April 1-9
Research	March 1
Books checked out of library	February 28

The students quickly realized that they must obtain their books right away. Even though the due date for the completed project was four and one-half months away, they could see that they needed every bit of the time.

This method of planning accomplishes three goals:

#1 It creates an urgency to complete the work and stay on task.

#2 It teaches students to plan for success.

#3 Students pay closer attention to the due dates because they scheduled them.

If you discuss all aspects of the assignment, they will **not** have to rely on parents to tell them when and how to do the project. It also eliminates procrastination. I believe most people procrastinate because they think they have more time than they do and fail to realize how much time is required for a project. Students can easily plan other projects in the same fashion.

Offer your students the opportunity to have their work checked before it is due to see if they are on the right track. Give them a "heads up" on how successful students get the most out of every project. By turning in their papers early, they will know if they need to make changes. Too many students wait for the due date instead of using this method to improve.

This method is one that older students continue to use. They return to report that they avoided a "C" on a paper simply by turning it in early. My younger daughter turned in what she thought was an "A" paper to her freshman professor. She submitted it early and it was returned covered with red marks. Although devastated, she made the suggested corrections. She earned an "A" on the final paper.

Consider the attention students pay to errors if they are able to make corrections before a grade is given. Since they are giving their full attention to making corrections, they learn from their mistakes. How much time does the typical student spend looking at the corrections on a "C" paper? None. Many times "C" papers are thrown away without a second glance. The benefit of turning an assignment in early is the learning that occurs as part of the process.

Failing to Plan is Planning to Fail

Chapter 24

Creating a Safe Environment

Every student failure is an opportunity. We set the stage for the way students feel about mistakes by our responses to them. Students bring many experiences with them when they begin a program of this nature. They carry reactions from previous teachers as well as the attitudes of their parents. It is not uncommon for parents to speak for their students because of the fears they carry from their own childhoods. They remember having been afraid to ask the teacher a question for fear of appearing stupid, so they pass this anxiety on to their students. For this reason there are a few things we need to do to assure that our students feel comfortable coming to us.

"There is no such thing as a stupid question" is a statement I have heard many teachers share with their students. However, teachers convey the opposite belief by their facial expressions and negative comments. If we want students to gain from this program, they must feel free to ask questions. It is important to let students know that even if you have a funny look on your face, it doesn't mean you do not value their questions.

Kevin's mother approached me one afternoon to inform me that he thought I didn't like him. This was a strange comment, considering he was a student I thoroughly enjoyed having in class. He asked amazing questions and took our discussions in interesting directions. I learned much from him that year. The three of us met to clear up this misconception. The following dialogue ensued:

"Kevin, I understand that you are confused as to how I feel about you. I want to assure you that I value you very much and enjoy having you in class. I am curious. What is it that made you feel I don't like you? Your answer could help me be a better teacher."

"Well, you know when I asked a question about the Indians? You had a funny look on your face."

"Kevin, I think I remember the situation you are talking about. Was it on the day I told the class that I had a headache?"

"It could have been."

"Well, when you asked the question I was probably thinking, 'Why did I come to school today? My head is killing me.'"

"I thought you were mad at me."

"I am glad you shared this with me. What I would like you to do in the future is to continue asking your great questions and don't be too concerned with the look on your teachers' faces. He or she may not be feeling well."

This situation made it clear that maintaining open communication is imperative to success. It also validated the need for students to be able to interpret my reactions. The balloon demonstration described below helps students do just that.

When an irritation occurs it is like adding air to a balloon. As more irritations occur, the balloon begins to fill. A student can drop a pencil box and set the teacher off because she is already dealing with a full balloon. Students remember home situations when their mothers reacted to what appeared to be nothing. They quickly recognize that their mothers' balloons were full.

In September, I announce that I will tell the class whenever I have a full balloon. This prevents it from exploding. Communicating our feelings is important. We do not want students to misinterpret our facial expressions.

Food for Thought

Educators have the opportunity to try a variety of methods. If one doesn't work, we try another. If we teach the same grade level for several years, we have the chance to reinvent the wheel every year. Our students do not have the same advantage. If they do poorly on a test in September, their grade reflects it in January, even if they have improved.

Consider offering your students opportunities to improve performance on worksheets, tests and quizzes. Allowing them to improve their grades by finding out what they did not know is learning at its best.

Supply List

Three-Ring Binder
Agenda
Highlighter, preferably yellow
Green Pen, a learning pen for indicating what students learn from their mistakes
Extra Paper
Zipper Pouch
Magic Rub Eraser
Sheet Protectors for Test Practice
Washable Overhead Projector Pens
Colored Felt Pens
Colored Pencils
Note cards
Graph Paper
Squeezies
Gum if necessary
Hard rubber tubbing for chewing

Chapter 25

Study Tools

Note cards: Note cards make great flash cards for vocabulary or remembering key points. They should be created as the student reads. The kinesthetic manner of recording the information is the first step in remembering. It is more valuable for students to write the flash cards themselves than to be given prepared cards. If they use another student's cards, they miss the first step in studying and will not get the same benefit from the cards.

Outlines: Outlines help students focus on the main ideas of a chapter or lecture. When lecturing, it is helpful to point out the key ideas students should record on the outline. Providing a prepared outline will not offer the same benefits as when students create their own. If students need help, you can provide them with a skeleton outline and ask them to fill in the blanks.

Acetate, overhead erasable pens: These can be used with blank diagrams, models, worksheets, timed tests, cursive writing pages or maps. The acetate or page protectors (non-shiny) allow students to test themselves on parts of a diagram or any fill-in page. Because the plastic sheets can be erased, they are a great way to get practice without making extra copies of worksheets or tests. This process can also be self correcting for the student.

Music and Dance: Creating a song or dance to help remember important information is very helpful for some students.

Poems: Rhyming often makes information easier to remember.

Discussion groups: For the social student, discussion groups are great. Students can read together and ask each other questions. If they are verbal, this will reinforce the information because articulated information reaches their long-term memories.

Sticky notes: Using sticky notes to record important information aids students as they read.

- They can be used as flash cards after the reading is completed.
- They can help students answer questions at the end of each chapter.
- They are helpful when reading a novel. Students can keep track of the

plot and characters without having to reread the book.
They are a wonderful way to get all students involved in classroom discussion. When I ask a question, I have each student write the answer on a sticky note. When everyone has recorded an answer, we share the ideas. This allows thinking time for all students and doesn't permit passive listeners to depend on their peers.

• They make great organizers for stories. I encourage students to brainstorm ideas on the sticky notes and then organize them in a sequence that makes sense. Doing this on a bedroom wall is a wonderful way to view all the ideas, step back and see how they fit together.

• The notes help a student who shouts out in class. He can get a thought out immediately by writing it down.

• When a student has a question when you are in the middle of another explanation, recording the question on a sticky note will allow the student to focus on your answer to another student's question. Otherwise, he is so focused on his own question that he does not hear anything else.

Charts: Charts help students organize information for comparing and contrasting. They need this approach modeled.

Studying math facts:

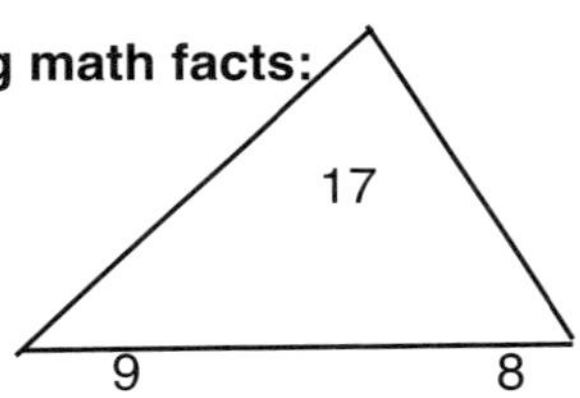

Studying math facts is more efficient if the fact is seen as one unit. What do you remember when you look at a flashcard missing an answer? You see a blank. Using visual memory to retrieve information requires students to look at the pattern as a combination of three numbers so they can insert the missing piece.

By practicing the patterns 9, 8, 17; 8, 9, 17; 17, 8, 9 and 17, 9, 8, students can easily read the following patterns and fill in the **missing numbers:**

17	17	9	8
- 9	-8	+8	**+9**

Instead of reading the problem as 17 minus 9, students read 17, 9, (blank) and the missing number will come easily.

Graph paper: Visual spatial students benefit from seeing their spelling and vocabulary words written on graph paper. By creating a picture of the configuration of the word, they can determine if the word is spelled correctly from visual clues. It can also be helpful for organizing math problems, outlining, time lines, semantic mapping or graphing.

Color: Crayons, markers and dry erase boards

Color is very helpful for visual learners. Creating flow charts, graphs or simply writing groupings in the same color are helpful study tools. Incorporating color on index cards will improve the visual learner's memory. If students are required to know the part of speech along with the definition of the word, they can write vocabulary words in code. The verbs can be green, the nouns red, the adjectives orange and the adverbs blue. Students will remember the color of the word and since blue and green are complimentary colors, they will signal that the verb and adverb go together.

This method can be applied to history and science concepts as well. Using different color cards will also help organize similar concepts.

Drawings: Create a drawing that depicts the concept you are learning. One picture is worth a thousand words. Stick figures can tell a lot and trigger your memory.

Graphomotor Memory Development

Students with spelling difficulties will benefit from short but frequent experiences with writing spelling words. This will help them develop kinesthetic memory of the word. If cursive has been introduced, it can give students a sense of the flow of the word. The writing of the word is not broken but creates a continuous flow. Practice will help students determine if this is an effective method for them. If the words are practiced over a period of time, students will develop motor memory and will not have to concentrate on the isolated letters. With enough practice, students can close their eyes and write the word. This can be accomplished by following these guidelines:

1. Practice writing the word twice a day. Allow time between writing sessions. Do this daily from the day the words are introduced until the day of the test. This method helps students build a long-term memory of the word's formation.
2. Students will concentrate on the formation of the word and its correct spelling.
3. Students can place their papers on top of a stack of newsprint to help reinforce the motor memory of writing the word.
4. Using a soft lead pencil will give students more friction, which helps memory.

But wait, there's more...
The following books are available at www.homeworkdoc.com

Homework Solutions: A Parent's Guide
The Missing Link Between Home and School
2nd Edition

This book offers strategies for parents. Parents are doing their best, if they knew how to do it differently they would. The strategies in this book offer alternatives. As they read, their thinking shifts and they see options available to them that they didn't realized existed. It's an empowering book for parents, helping them create students who are self-advocates.

Homework Solutions for Weary Students and Their Parents

After reading *Homework Solutions: A Parent's Guide*, parents requested more words to empower their children to become self advocates. Ms. Olivadoti's third grade class experienced thirty-nine challenges in one year; the solutions are provided in this book. Written at a third grade reading level, this book is ideal for use by students of any age. Many college students comment that they wished they had learned this material long before they entered college.

Homework Solutions: A Curriculum for Success

This book offers schools a kindergarten through eighth grade curriculum designed to develop independent and self-reliant students. It is available at www.homeworkdoc.com as a downloadable file.

Try Its

Record Questions for the Homework Doc:

About the Author

By Shelly Olivadoti

Victoria Olivadoti resides in Fountain Valley, California and teaches in Huntington Beach, California. She also serves as a consultant to school districts, teachers, students, parents and colleges. She is a guest columnist as the 'Homework Doc' for the *Long Beach Grunion Gazette*.

Ms. Olivadoti's 35-year career includes extensive experience teaching children of varied educational backgrounds, ages and skill levels. She also successfully guided my sister and me through school using the tools described here. This book and her earlier books reflect her enthusiasm for teaching and her altruistic nature.

The "Homework Solutions" series is the result of her ability to recognize a challenge and meet it. She has created solutions for parents and teachers nationwide to help their children and for students across the U.S. to be successful in school and life.

Ms. Olivadoti's Pledge to You

By purchasing this book, you are entitled to free on-line help. Email your questions or challenges to Ms. Olivadoti at
tolivadoti@aol.com
or vicki@homeworkdoc.com

Ms. Olivadoti Presents

Invite Ms. Olivadoti to your school for one or more of her powerful seminars to strengthen student achievement.

Three seminars are available:

Educator, Parent and Student

New!

Living Room Dialogues- Invite friends in for a night of problem solving in the comfort of your home.

Contact her today for details at

714 964-6353

tolivadoti@aol.com

vicki@homeworkdoc.com

Visit www.homeworkdoc.com
for FREE downloads